Pennsylvania State Notary Public Study Guide and Exam Prep

2023-2024

MOST COMPREHENSIVE AND UP-TO-DATE GUIDE WITH 9 PRACTICE TESTS!

Henry Foreman

&

Morris Test PC

D1527955

COVER DESIGN

JENNIFER LAWRENCE

FIRST EDITION

Contents

Introduction

Becoming a notary can be either a career choice or a side job to help you pay some extra bills. No matter what reason you have for becoming a notary, you are going to need to go through several steps to become a notary. In most states, it is a process of paying fees and filling out applications. However, there are some states where you have to take educational courses and pass an exam. In this book, we are first going to briefly look at the job of a notary and what it entails. Then we're going to help you prepare for the notary exam by giving you some practice tests.

Part 1: General Notary Exam Prep

What is a Notary?

A notary is an official who is appointed by the state government to serve the public as an impartial witness when it comes to completing a variety of official fraud-deterrent acts linked to signing important documents. The official acts are referred to as notarizations or notarial acts. Notaries are commissioned publicly as "ministerial" officials, which means they need to follow written rules without significant personal discretion.

The duty of a notary is to screen those who are signing important documents to ensure their true identity, their willingness to sign without intimidation or duress and their awareness of the transaction or document. Some notarizations will also require the notary to put the signer under oath, declaration under penalty of perjury that the information in the document is true and correct. Some documents that typically require a notary include property deeds, wills and powers of attorney.

The foundation of the notary's public trust is impartiality. A notary is duty-bound not to act in situations if they have a personal interest. The public trust that the notary's screening tasks aren't corrupted by self-interest. Impartiality also dictates that a notary won't refuse to serve someone based on race, nationality, religion, politics, sexual orientation or status.

Since the notary is an official representative of the state, they will certify the proper execution of many life-changing documents related to private citizens. Whether these documents are real estate, grant powers of attorney, establish a prenuptial agreement or perform other activities related to the functioning of civil society.

Notaries and the notarization process are responsible for deterring fraud and establishing that individuals know the document they are signing and are willing participants in the transaction.

A notary will often ask to see a current ID with a photo, physical description and signature. This is often a driver's license or passport. This will help establish a person's identity before signing a document.

A notary in the United States is different from those in other countries. In the United States, a notary is not an attorney, judge or other high-ranking official. The biggest confusion comes from Notario Publico in other countries, which can make it confusing for immigrants. For this reason, notaries in the United States need to be very clear about what they can and cannot do.

Those who are interested can become a notary in their home state by meeting eligibility requirements and following the necessary steps for the commissioning process. Each state has its own process, but in general, you will fill out an application and pay a state application fee. In some states, you'll also need to take a training course or pass an exam.

Before we look more at the process of becoming a notary, let's take a moment to look more at the notarization process.

What is Notarization?

Notarization is a fraud-deterrent process that assures a document is authentic and trustworthy and all parties in the transaction are aware. The notary public that performs the process uses a three-part system: vetting, certifying and record-keeping. Notarizations are often referred to as "notarial acts." The notary public is a duly appointed and impartial individual who assures that a document is authentic with a genuine signature done without duress or intimidation to ensure the terms of the document can be in full effect. The main value of notarization is the impartial screening of the signer when it comes to identity, willingness and awareness. The notary is essentially protecting the personal rights and property of people from forgers, identity thieves and others looking to exploit vulnerable individuals. Let's take a moment to consider the different notarial acts.

Acknowledgments

These are often performed on documents that control or convey ownership of valuable assets. This would include documents such as property deeds, powers of attorney and trusts. For these documents, the signer needs to appear in person and be positively identified in order to declare or acknowledge that the signature is their own and that the provisions of the document can take effect just as they are written.

Jurats

This is typically performed on evidentiary documents involved in the operation of the civil and criminal justice system. This would include documents such as affidavits, depositions and interrogatories. For these documents, a signer needs to appear in person and speak aloud an oath or affirmation of the truth of the statements in the document. The person who takes the oath or affirmation can be prosecuted for perjury if they don't remain truthful.

Certified Copies

This is done to confirm a reproduction of an original is

true, exact and complete. This would include documents like college degrees, passports and other one-and-only personal papers that can't be copy-certified by a public record office like the bureau of vital statistics. This notarization isn't an authorized notarial act in all states, and in the states where it is allowed, it can only be done with certain types of original documents.

Each state has its own laws when it comes to performing notarial acts. While different, these laws are mostly congruent with most common notarizations.

Parts of a Notarization

The first part of a notarization is the notary's screening of the signer for identity, volition and awareness.

The second part of the process is to enter the key details in the "journal of notarial acts." A chronological journal is considered the best practice, but it isn't required by law. In some states, there is a requirement for document signers to provide a signature and thumbprint in the notary's journal.

The third part is the completion of a "notarial

certificate" that states which facts are being certified by the notary. The climax is the affixation of the notary's signature and seal of office to the certificate. The seal is a universally recognized symbol and provides the document weight in legal matters since it is made genuine in view of the court of law.

Now that we know what a notary is and how the process of notarization occurs. Let's take a moment to consider why you should consider becoming a notary.

Why Become a Notary

Millions of people have chosen to become notaries, and it remains a high-demand business. While being a notary may not seem like a big deal, they hold a lot of power in the legal community. Becoming a notary is also a great way to have some side income or improve your resume. Let's consider five of the top reasons why you should consider becoming a notary.

Additional Source of Income

Although appointed by the state and serving as a

public official, notaries charge clients directly and get to keep their revenue. This is why many communities have people who serve as mobile notaries. States often regulate how much a notary charges for individual notarizations, but clients will often need more than one signature notarized. Additional fees can also be charged, such as travel, supplies and other expenses.

Notary Signing Agent Certification

If you want to become a notary to have some additional income, then you should consider becoming a notary signing agent or NSA. An NSA is a certified and trained professional that notarizes loan documents in real estate closings. NSAs are the main link between banks and borrowers in order to complete the loan. These notaries are hired by title companies directly, but their services are done as an independent contractor to ensure the loan documents are signed by the borrower, notarized and returned for processing. This line of work increases the income a person can get from notary work.

Resume and Skill Improvement

A variety of industries use the services of a notary,

including banking, finance, medical, legal, government, insurance and even technology. If you become a notary, then you'll be adding to your skill set and can improve your resume while increasing your employee value. From an employer standpoint, notaries serve two main functions: they can notarize documents for co-workers and bosses or for customers. A lot of employers value an employee with notary skills in order to handle all document authentication needs and provide additional services to customers.

Keep a Flexible Schedule

If you choose to become a notary, you can enjoy the flexibility of setting your own work schedule. A notary is a perfect job for home-based workers and those who want a job that fits their schedule. In addition, most people who need the services of a notary request them after normal business hours, so you can easily arrange a time that works best for you.

Provide a Community Resource

Notaries are known for helping people in need. If you want to give back to your community, then being a notary is a great choice. Often people need the services of a notary but can't afford the cost, such as the elderly, homeless and college students. These people often need powers of attorney, residency affidavits, advanced medical directives, college transcripts and enrollment verifications, to name a few. Notaries often set aside some time to work from community centers, retirement homes and campuses with free or low-cost notarizations. It can even be a way to market your services and network for paying clients.

If any of these situations seem appealing to you, then you should definitely look into becoming a notary. To do so, you need to be aware of the general requirements needed to become a notary. Let's take a moment to consider the general requirements of a notary before we start looking at specifics.□

General Notary Requirements

Although the process for becoming a notary varies based on the state you live in, the general requirements and steps for becoming a notary are the following:

- Ensure you can meet all the qualifications of your state.

- Complete an application and submit it to the appropriate state department.

- Pay any required state filing fee.

- If needed, start training from an approved educational vendor.

- If needed, pass a state-administered exam.

- If needed, complete a background check and fingerprinting.

- Receive a commission certificate from the state.

- If needed, get a surety bond.

- File commission paperwork and bond, if required, with the notary regulating official in your state.

- Buy necessary notary supplies.

Let's look a little closer at the process of notary training. This isn't required in all states, but several states do require notaries to complete training before they can get certified.

Notary Training

Notary training is required in the following states:

- California

- Colorado

- Florida

- Missouri

- Montana

- Nevada

- North Carolina

- Ohio

- Oregon

- Pennsylvania

Delaware requires training and continuing education for electronic notaries only.

Notary training needs to be approved by the state, so as long as you sign up for an approved course, you'll be covering the required basics during training. Although not many states require a notary to be trained, most states will support an individual's voluntary education.

If you want to undergo voluntary education, you should check with the notary regulating agency for your state. This is often the Secretary of State's office. Some community colleges will also provide educational courses. There are also a number of online organizations and vendors who will provide notary education. Most of these courses are going to provide practical information that helps you to learn how to perform your official duties.

Whether online or in the classroom, training courses will often take about three to six hours. However, optional training can fall outside of these parameters. There is also no official standard for the cost of notary training, so the cost can vary based on the provider. Online training is often going to cost less than $100, while classroom training typically costs between $100 and $200.

In addition to training, some states will also require individuals to take an exam in order to become a notary.

Notary Exam

Most states don't require a notary exam in order to get certified. The following states require a notary exam:

- California

- Colorado

- Connecticut

- Hawaii

- Louisiana

- Maine

- Montana

- Nebraska

- New York

- North Carolina

- Ohio

- Oregon

- Utah

Wyoming encourages individuals to take an at-home test but doesn't currently require it.

The notary exam takes about an hour. Some exams may require the submission of fingerprints with the state application at the end of the exam.

Another general requirement to become a notary is to have the appropriate bond and insurance.

Notary Bonds and Insurance

Most states require notaries to have a bond and insurance. In fact, thirty states and the District of Columbia require notaries to have a surety bond. The difference is the amount required by the state. The typical amount ranges from $5,000 to $10,000, but the lowest is $500, and the highest is $25,000. The surety bond helps to protect consumers. Should the notary make a mistake that damages someone, the bond will compensate the injured person up to the amount of the bond. The notary is then required to repay the bond company.

Since state laws aren't written to protect notaries but rather the public, liability insurance isn't required by notaries. This is why states require bonds instead. However, individual notaries can choose to purchase errors and omissions insurance policies since they can protect them from claims related to errors made during a notarization.

The last general requirement to consider is the notary commission. After this, we can start looking at specific state requirements.

Notary Commission

Notaries are both regulated and commissioned at the state level. This is often done through the Secretary of State's Office, but in some states, this can also be done by the county clerk or another governing body.

Depending on the requirements in your state, the process to become a notary can take seven to nine weeks. It can also take longer if the state is processing a lot of renewals. The shortest it can take is four weeks if your state has minimal requirements.

Most states have organizations that can help you with the process of becoming a notary. It can be a good idea to use one of these organizations since there are multiple steps that need to be completed in an appropriate order. In Florida, Illinois, and Texas, you are required to use specific vendors, and you can't apply yourself directly.

In most states, once you are certified, you can notarize documents throughout the state. Some states do have unique rules when it comes to jurisdiction. This can limit where you are allowed to notarize within the state or perform notarizations for citizens that don't live in the state.

You should be able to notarize for anyone with a legitimate and legal request with acceptable identification. The main restriction in some states is limiting staff notaries to business-related documents during business hours when employed by a business.

The typical term for a notary is four years, but it can vary by state. Some states can also have five and ten-year terms.

The reason for the difference in requirements is that notaries are commissioned and overseen by individual states. Since state notary laws are different, the requirements can also vary greatly. For example, in California, most notary laws are in place because of lawsuits and public damage.

Now that we have an understanding of the general requirements to become a notary, let's get a little more specific. As we've already shown, most states don't require an exam. It is always a good idea to study the general rules and regulations for all notaries, as this is often the bulk of exam questions. Take a moment to consider some practice questions that can help you with the general rules and regulations for a notary.

What You Should Know

Before you take your notary exam, there are some general things you should know. While only a few states require a notary exam, fewer states actually require you to know things specific to their state. In general, most state exams are only going to ask general questions related to all notaries throughout the United States. For this reason, to help you pass your notary exam, we are going to review some key points and general notary requirements, the basic rules and exceptions, the common fines and penalties, and some key points to remember before taking your exam. Then we'll also go over some general tips to help you have the easiest time taking your notary exam.

Key Point and General Notary Requirements

- Notary commissions are valid for four years.

- Notaries can perform notarial acts anywhere within the boundaries of their state.

- Notaries need to clear a background check by having a Live Scan Fingerprinting done before they receive their commission.

- Certain actions will prevent a notary from being commissioned:

  o Failing to disclose convictions and/or arrests on the application.

  o A felony conviction within the last ten years of probation.

  o A misdemeanor conviction within the last five years of probation completion.

○ Not complying with family and child support obligations.

• Notaries are not allowed to provide legal advice about immigration or other legal matters unless they are a practicing attorney who has passed the state bar.

• Laws require a notary to perform notarizations if a proper request is made.

• Any documents that involve real property and powers of attorney require the notary to obtain a right thumbprint.

• Notarial acts and procedures include the following:

○ Acknowledgements

○ Jurats

○ Signature by Mark

○ Proof of Execution by Subscribing to Witness Certificates

○ Certified Copies of Power of Attorney

○ Certified Copies of the Notary's Journal

• In order for a document to be notarized, it needs to meet three criteria:

○ The document must be complete.

○ The document must contain the signature of the principal.

○ The document must have the correct notarial wording.

• Notarial Acts can only be completed by the notary and not the signer.

• Notarial wording can appear on the document or on a loose-leaf certificate.

• The four-step process for performing a notarization needs to be completed in entirety:

○ Identifying the signer.

○ Completing the journal entry.

○ Signing by the principal/signer and using the right

thumbprint when necessary.

○ Fill out the notarial act/wording.

• The notary's sequential journal and seal/stamp need to be kept under the exclusive and direct control of the notary.

Notary Rules and/or Exceptions

• Signers must be identified through Satisfactory Evidence, which is done through one of three processes:

○ Specific Paper Identification Documents

○ Oath of a Single Credible Witness

○ Oath of Two Credible Witnesses

• The maximum fee a notary can charge is $15, with the following exceptions:

○ Depositions can charge $30, with the administration of oath being $7 and the certificate to the deposition another $7. But never higher than a charge of $44.

• The signer of the document needs to personally

appear before the notary in order for their signature to be notarized. With the following exceptions:

o A subscribing witness can be used when a signer has another person prove to the notary that they signed the document.

• Signers need to sign both the document and the notary journal. With the following exceptions:

o A signature by mark can occur when the signer is unable to sign or write their name. The signer should have the document notarized by marking a mark in the presence of two witnesses.

• A notary notarizes signatures, but they don't certify documents. With the following two exceptions:

o Copies of the notary's own journal.

o Copies of a Power of Attorney.

• Notaries have a 30-day rule to reply to the Secretary of State with three exceptions:

o If their stamp/seal is lost or stolen, then an

immediate reply is warranted.

○ If their journal is lost or stolen, then an immediate reply is warranted.

○ If their journal is taken by a peace officer, then a ten-day reply is warranted.

• The notary must use their stamp/seal on all notarized documents, with the exception of Subdivision Maps.

• A notaries seal/stamp can't be surrendered to anyone with the following exceptions:

○ A court/judge can require the surrender of the seal/stamp after a commission is revoked when the notary is convicted of a crime related to Notarial Misconduct, including the false completion of a notarial certificate or a felony. In this instance, two things must be noted.

■ The court/judge forwards the seal to the Secretary of State with a certified copy of the conviction judgment.

■ This is the only time someone is allowed to possess the notary seal since you need to destroy the notary seal when the commission is no longer valid.

- The journal needs to be kept under the notary's exclusive and personal control at all times. No one is allowed access to the information in the journal, with the following exceptions:

  o Members of the public can get a lined item copy of the journal with a written request.

  o Under a court order, the examination and copying of the journal can be done in the notary's presence.

  o An employer can perform a business examination and copying of the journal in the presence of the notary.

Common Fines and Penalties

- A $75,000 fine is applied in the following circumstance:

  o Deed of Trust Fraud. This is the willful fraud and false filings in connection with a Deed of Trust on a Single-Family Residence.

- $10,000 penalties occur in two situations:

  o Identity of the Credible Witness. This is the failure to

obtain the satisfactory evidence needed to establish the identity of a single credible witness.

○ Penalty of Perjury/Acknowledgement. This is when someone willfully states as true a material fact and/or falsifies a certificate of acknowledgment.

• $2,500 civil penalties can be applied in two circumstances:

○ Failing to provide a notary journal to a peace office when requested.

○ Failing to obtain the required thumbprint.

• $1,500 violations are willful and intentional violations. They can be the following:

○ Using false or misleading advertising where the notary public represents that they have duties, rights or privileges that they don't possess.

○ Committing any act that involves dishonesty, fraud or notarial misconduct.

○ Executing any certificate as a notary that contains a

statement known to be false to the notary.

o Violating the prohibition against a notary who holds themselves as an immigration specialist or consultant advertising or

■ Violating the restrictions on charging to assist in completing immigration forms and

■ Violating the restrictions on advertising notarial services in a language other than English

o Translating the words "notary public" into Spanish.

o Failing to fully and faithfully discharge any of the duties or responsibilities required of a notary public.

o Unauthorized manufacturing, duplicating or selling the public seal of a notary.

o Failing to notify the Secretary of State that a public seal is lost, stolen, destroyed or damaged.

• $1,000 fine is applied in the following situation:

o Unlawful Practice of Law. This is when any person is

practicing law but is not an active member of the State Bar.

- $750 violations are not willful oversights that can still be considered violations. This includes the following:

  ○ Failing to discharge notary duties.

  ○ Charging more than the prescribed fees stated by notary law.

  ○ Failing to complete the acknowledgment at the time the signature and seal are affixed to the document.

  ○ Failing to administer the oath or affirmation as required.

  ○ Accepting improper identification.

- $500 infraction penalties apply in the following situation:

  ○ Failing to notify the Secretary of State in two situations

    ■ Changing a business, mailing or residential address

and

■ Changing the name of the notary public.

Along with these penalties, a denial of an application or suspension or revocation of the notary commission can occur. If a person is guilty of a misdemeanor and/or felony, they can also be liable in a civil action for damages.

Key Points to Know

• Certain notarial acts require specific wording. This includes the following:

○ For an acknowledgment, the following specifics are needed:

■ This is the most common form of notarization

■ It must be done in the notary's presence

■ The notary needs to positively identify the signer

■ The signer needs to acknowledge signing the document

■ Out-of-state acknowledgments are allowed as long as the certification doesn't require the notary to supersede the notarial law in their practicing state

○ For a jurat, the following specifics are needed:

■ This is the second most common form of notarization.

■ The signer must sign the document in the notary's presence.

■ The notary must administer a separate oath for each jurat.

■ Out-of-state jurats aren't acceptable, and a loose-leaf jurat needs to be used.

○ For proof of execution by a subscribing witness certificate, the following specifics are needed:

■ This document is used when the document principal/signer can't personally appear before the notary.

■ This document can't be used on any documents that affect real property or on documents that require a thumbprint in the notary's journal.

■ The subscribing witness needs to be identified by a credible witness with an acceptable form of identification.

■ There has to be an unbroken chain of personal knowledge:

• The notary needs to know the credible witness, the credible witness needs to know the subscribing witness and the subscribing witness needs to know the principal.

• Notaries are allowed to notarize documents in any language they can't speak or read since they aren't responsible for the contents of the documents, provided the notarial wording is in English.

• Notaries can't notarize documents for a signer that they are unable to communicate. And they can't use an interpreter.

• When completing a notarization with a signature by mark, the following applies:

○ The process requires two viewing witnesses who observe the principal/signer making their mark on the document and in the notary's journal.

○ The viewing witnesses don't have to be identified, but they do need the following:

■ They must sign the document as witnesses.

■ The witness must cursive the principal/signer's name next to the mark on the document.

■ The witness or the notary needs to write the principal/signer's name next to the mark in the notary's journal.

• The notary must take, subscribe and file the oath of office and file a surety bond with the county clerk's office or place of business as stated in the application within 30 calendar days from the date of the commission.

• Errors and Omissions Insurance can be purchased to protect a notary who damages someone as a result of notarial misconduct or negligence. This can even be true in the following situations:

○ Even simple oversights like failing to affix a notary seal or properly identify a principal/signer can subject the notary to being personally liable for losses and/or damages.

- A notary public is allowed to notarize for relatives as long as don't so doesn't provide a direct financial or beneficial interest to the notary.

- The employer of a notary can limit notarization to the following in the ordinary course of employment:

  ○ Who and when to notarize and

  ○ How much the notary can charge for their services

- Notaries are prohibited from providing legal advice and/or practice law unless they are also a licensed and practicing attorney.

These are the general facts that apply to notaries in all states. This information forms the basics of what is covered in most notary exams in states that require them. Knowing this information is the first step in helping you pass your notary exams. The next thing you need to do is prepare for your notary exam. Even in states where the exam is a handful of open-book questions, it can be a good idea to prepare and study in advance. Let's consider some practical tips to help you study for and prepare to take the notary exam.

Preparing for the Notary Exam

The notary public is responsible for verifying signatures on important legal and real estate documents. Most states require notaries to have some level of education before getting a commission, and a few states require individuals to take a licensing exam in order to show they understand the basic knowledge of notary laws and the role they play in society. Tests are often done at testing centers in written form or online, and the exact requirements will vary by state. You'll often have plenty of time to prepare for your exam, and the following are some tips to help you prepare for the notary exam if it is required in your state.

Study Guides and Handbooks

The licensing authority of the state in which you want to serve as a notary public will provide guidelines for taking the exam. This will often include a handbook. The handbook for the state will provide all aspects of becoming a notary public, the laws that need to be followed and the specific duties of a notary public as allowed in that state. By studying these handbooks, you can get a good idea of what specific state information may be on the exam in addition to the general guidelines and information we listed above.

Review Notary Public Laws and Recent Cases

You can also research online about notary public laws for your state. This can often be found online at the state legislature home page and a search of the words notary public. This will be the easiest way to find the most recent applicable legislation. The full texts of the laws are often available on the website of the agencies that issue licenses. For example, the Secretary of State in New York provides full texts of their laws online. You can also search for recent court cases that involve potential errors by notaries public so you can have some real-life examples of the application of notary laws.

Study Potential Scenarios

Take a moment to look up frequently asked questions and common requests for notaries. Many state agencies that license notaries will have this information on their websites. For example, California offers these questions and their associated answers online. Playing out potential scenarios is a great way to help you understand the laws and the appropriate actions you should take. This practice can help you when it comes to answering multiple-choice questions related to the decision-making process of notaries. For example, as a notary, you may be asked to notarize a document that you didn't personally view the signing of and choosing the right action in the situation can be a real question on an exam.

Test Questions and Practice Tests

The last thing you can do is consider taking practice tests and questions. Self-testing can help you check your research and see what areas you need to increase your research. There are paid practice tests you can take online, but for a simple general question test, you can often do this on your own with a few sample questions, such as you'll get in the upcoming practice tests of this book.

All of these things are going to help you prepare for your notary exam. Now let's provide you with some practice tests to get ready for your notary exam. First, we'll provide some general notary exam practice questions and answers for you to prepare with, then we'll look at some specific examples of questions.

Part 2: Pennsylvania Notary Public Exam Study Guide

This is a guidebook to assist you with the Notary Public Exam in Pennsylvania. The formal booklet is available online but contains a huge amount of legal jargon and confusing terminology. Here we have simplified the text and highlighted what you MUST know for the exam. In addition, we have provided the most common questions that are most likely to be asked in the test. The Commonwealth of Pennsylvania places a heavy emphasis on definitions, and it is important to know the meaning of all the legal terms in the text below.

Qualifications

- Be at least 18 years of age

- Be able to read and write English

- Be employed or a resident of the Commonwealth

- Be a permanent resident or a citizen (one cannot be an illegal or undocumented immigrant)

- Complete an approved 3-hour basic education notary course

- Pass the notary public exam

- Submit proof of the completed certificate of the basic education course with a notary public application

- Not have any notary public commission revoked by the Commonwealth or any other state

- Not have any prior convictions, especially felony

Who is not Eligible To Apply?

1. Any individual holding a judicial office in the Commonwealth, except the office of justice of peace, alderman, or magistrate

2. All members of Congress and any individual holding any office or appointment or trust under the executive, legislative, and judiciary Departments of the US Govt, and they are salaried.

3. Any member of the General Assembly of PA

Steps for Initial Appointment

1. First, complete a 3-hour notary education course. The application must be submitted with proof of completion of the basic education course.

2. The study course must be completed within six months of submitting the application.

3. There is a non-refundable fee of $42

4. Complete and pass the state exam. The state exam results are valid for one year. The test may be retaken as

often as needed within a six month period.

5. After passing the state exam, you will be issued an appointment letter and a blank bond. The Dept will send the commission certificate to the Recorder of deeds office in the county where the notary is employed or has an office.

6. The notary public must obtain a notary bond within 45 days of the appointment in the amount of $10K. The bond is usually available from an authorized insurer in the state and covers notary acts performed during the commission period.

7. Next, the notary public has to provide his or her signature and take the oath of office before the Recorder of deeds (Within 45 days). He will then receive the commission certificate from the Recorder of deeds.

8. The notary should register an official signature in the prothonotary's office within 45 days. The Dept will then issue a commission that is good for four years.

Renewal Requirements

1. The initial appointment is good for four years.

2. If the commission is expiring, the notary should reapply within 60 days of the expiration date.

3. All the same steps as the initial application are necessary, including taking the education notary course. Only no final notary exam is required as long as the commission has not expired.

Education

1. All applicants must pass an examination administered by the Dept or an entity approved by the Dept

2. Within six months of the application, the applicant must complete a 3-hour notary public basic education course

3. All notaries are required to complete an approved notary education course–there are no exceptions

Examination

1. Before the appointment, all applicants must first pass the Notary exam. This applies to both new

applicants and those whose commission has expired.

2. The results of the notary exam are valid for 12 months from the date the exam was taken.

3. To pass the notary public exam, the candidate needs a score of 75% or higher.

4. Applicants can retake the exam as many times as necessary within six months to pass.

5. Only one exam can be written in a 24-hour period.

6. The exam focuses on the rules that notary officers have to comply with, the fees, dates of important events, and ethics.

Change of Personal Information

The Notary public must notify the Department within 30 days of any information change that includes the following:

- Office address

- Legal name

- Home address

- Name of electronic notarization vendor

- Voluntary resignation-this notice must be submitted in writing and include the date of the change.

If there is a legal change in the name, the application must be accompanied by the marriage certificate, divorce decree, or court order. This name change must be filed in the county where the notary public has an office.

When there is a name change, the notary may continue with the same name in which he or she was commissioned until the expiration date; at the time of reapplication, one can request a formal name change and start using the new name.

If the notary public resigns, he/she must notify the Department in writing/electronic means within 30 days.

Notary Appointment

1. The Notary commission is for four years

2. Can practice anywhere in the Commonwealth of PA

Mandatory Requirements

When a new appointment is made, within 45 days, the notary public:

• Must subscribe and file for the oath of office

• Execute a $10,000 surety bond

• The new appointee needs to register his or her official signature with the prothonotary in the county where the business practice is located.

• Record the bond, Commission, and oath of office with the recorder of deeds

• The Commission will be invalid if any of the above requirements are not met within 45 days

Notary Public Application

1. A PA resident can use their home or office address on their application

2. Out-of-state residents must use the PA business address

3. All convictions must be stated

4. If the notary public has resigned, or if the Commission was revoked or suspended, it must be stated

5. Any previous disciplinary action has to be explained

6. Any Legal judgment has to be explained

7. The signature on the notary public application must match parts 1 and part 2 of the application

Notary Bond, Errors & Omission Insurance

Notary Bond

• The law requires all notary public to secure a $10,000 surety bond

• The bond is a fund that pays against claims made against the notary public.

• The Notary bond is not an insurance policy; it offers limited liability when the notary public is involved in misadventures.

• If a claim is made against the notary bond, the notary public is obligated by law to pay it back

• The notary can even be liable for extra costs like court costs, legal fees, and administrative fees.

• If the notary is at fault in a claim, he or she is liable for damages and will need to reimburse the company for any funds paid out.

Errors & Omissions Insurance

A notary public also has the option of purchasing Errors and Omissions Insurance. This policy protects the notary if there are any inadvertent omissions or errors or when an individual files a false claim against the notary.

E & O insurance benefits include the following:

• Covers defense costs

• There is no deductible

• Protects against errors and omissions

• Additional notaries also automatically covered under a blanket policy

• The employer is also covered under a blanket policy at no charge

• Insurance protects against liability for the duration of the notary commission

Notary Responsibilities

Appointment and Commissions Eligibility

- Be at least 18 years of age

- Be a citizen or permanent resident

- Be a resident, practice, or be employed in the commonwealth

- Be able to read and write English

- Have passed the basic education test

The Application and Approval of the Commission

- Be made to the Department.

- Be accompanied by a non-refundable fee of $42-this fee includes the notary public commission application and fee for the filing of the bond

- Once appointed, and before the commission can be issued, the applicant must execute an oath or affirmation of office

Certificate of Notarial Act

1. When a notarial act is performed, the final evidence is a certificate.

2. The certificate must be executed at the time of the notarial act

3. The certificate must be dated and signed.

4. It must identify the county and state where the

notary act is performed

5. Should contain the title of the office of notary officer

6. The notary public must sign with the same name as it appears on the commission or executes the notary public's electronic signature, which reflects the signature identified in the commission.

7. The certificate has to reveal the expiration date of the commission.

Bond

1. Following appointment and before the commission can be active, the individual must obtain a surety bond in the amount of $10K within 45 days.

2. The bond is executed by an insurance company authorized to do business in PA.

3. The bond will cover acts performed during the term of the notary public.

4. If the notary public violates the law, the surety or issuing entity will be held liable under the bond

5. If the issuing entity of the surety bonds decides to cancel the bond, it has to give the Department a 30-day notice.

6. The surety or issuing entity must notify the Department within 30 days after making a payment to a claimant.

7. The notary public can only perform notarial acts during the time the bond is valid.

Official Signature

1. Has to be registered for a fee of $0.50 in the Notary Register in the prothonotary's office

2. The signature has to be registered within 45 days of appointment or reappointment or within 30 days after moving to a different county.

3. In a county of second class, the official signature can be registered in the office of the clerk of courts.

Recording and Filing

1. Once appointed as a notary public but prior to

undertaking the duties of a notary office, the individual has to record the oath of office, commission and bond with the office of the recorder.

2. Following reappointment as a notary officer, the individual again has to record the oath of office, commission and bond with the office of the recorder.

3. In addition, within 90 days of recording, a copy of the oath of office, commission and bond has to be filed with the Department.

Prothonotary and Recorder of Deeds Registration

1. After executing the surety bond, the notary must record the commission, bond, and oath with the recorder of deeds within 45 days.

2. A Prothonotary is an officer who acts as the principal clerk of the court. All notaries must register with the protonotary.

3. There are some counties where the notary does not go to the prothonotary's office to register the signature but to the Recorder of Deeds.

Responsibilities and Duties

- Complete the Notarial certificate.

- Must contain all relevant information for each notarial act

- The official stamp can be affixed or stamped to the certificate near the signature or attached to or associated with an electronic record constraining the notary's signature.

- Securely attach the notarial certificate to a tangible record using staples or a grommet; One is not allowed to use paper clips, tape, or binder clips as they are not secure.

- When signing, the signature should be handwritten and eligible. If the signature is not legible, the name should be printed next to it.

- The Signature must be legible, recognizable, understandable, and readable.

Conflict of Interest

If the notary public or the wife has a direct or pecuniary interest, the notary should not perform a notarial act.

Notary Public Duties

The notarial act can include the following:

- Taking an acknowledgment

- Administer an oath or affirmation

- Attesting or witnessing a signature

- Certifying or attesting a copy or deposition

- Noting a protest of a negotiable instrument

Acknowledgment

1. When the client brings an executable document to notarize, the resulting notarial act is an acknowledgment.

2. Acknowledgment is the most common notarial act

performed by the notary officer. It is defined as a formal statement by a person who appears before a notary public and states that he or she is the person who has signed the instrument (document) and that the signing was done voluntarily and with proper authority.

3. The individual will also state that he or she knew what they were doing at the time.

4. The act is performed in the presence of a notary.

5. A notary public can only charge $5 for an acknowledgment and $2 for each additional name.

6. The Notary public must use satisfactory evidence to substantiate the individual's identity.

7. The signer must be physically present, and he or she must sign the document voluntarily. The notary will need to compare the signature with that of a photo ID.

Executable Documents

• The executable document records a transaction that needs to be carried through.

• When an executable document is signed, it causes something to happen.

• Examples of executable documents include a power of attorney, contracts, mortgage agreements, healthcare directives, and deeds.

Oath or Affirmation

Oath

• It is a formal declaration of truth or promise to perform an act truthfully and faithfully

• Calls upon a supreme being or sacred object as witness

Affirmation

• A solemn declaration is given instead of an oath

Process of Oath or Affirmation

• One duty of the notary public is to administer an oath or affirmation.

- An oath or affirmation may be verbal

- Individuals have to physically appear in front of the notary public.

- The notary will either have personal knowledge of the individual or use satisfactory evidence to determine the identity of the individual.

- A record with a written oath or affirmation has to be signed.

Three Purposes for Oath or Affirmation

- The statement is the truth

- The testimony given is true

- That the notary officer will conduct his or her duties with reasonable care and judgment

Acceptable Oath or Affirmation

1. The oath and affirmation can be written or verbal.

2. The transaction has to be recorded in the official

notary public journal

3. The Notary public can charge up to $5 for each oath/affirmation

Taking a Verification on Oath or Affirmation

1. Taking a verification of a statement on oath or affirmation is common in notary practice.

2. The individual usually states that the contents of the document are true.

3. The individual making the verification must appear in person

4. The notary must conclude from personal knowledge or satisfactory evidence that the individual is who he or she claims to be

5. The signature on the statement verified must be the signature of the individual- one can compare the signature to that on the photo ID.

Witnessing or Attesting to Signatures

1. Notaries can witness or attest to an individual signing his or her name on a document

2. The record must be signed in the presence of the notary, but first, the ID of the individual needs to be verified

3. The signer signs and does not need to swear that the contents of the record are true

4. A notary public can charge up to $5 per signature

Certified or Attested Copies and Deposition

1. Notaries can certify a copy of a record.

2. The notary public must be presented with the original item to compare it to the copy.

3. When issuing a certified or attested copy, the notary public does not guarantee the authenticity of the original item or its contents.

Documents That Cannot be Notarized

Certain documents which notaries are not permitted to issue certified copies

- Birth and death certificates

- US naturalization certificates

- Any government document that says do not copy

- Any other record that is illegal to certify or copy

The notary public can issue certified copies of the following:

- Public Records

- Driver license

- Passport

- Diplomas

- Transcripts

- Leases

- Contracts

- Bill of Sale

- Medical records

- Power of attorney

Apostille

1. If the document is for overseas use, it will require an apostille or certification from the US State Dept or Pennsylvania Dept of State.

2. The notary public can charge up to $5 for each certification of a copy of the record.

Sign, Defined

1. Execution or adoption of a tangible symbol or mark

2. It is attached or associated with the recording of an electronic symbol, sound, or process.

Stamping Device

1. A physical item capable of affixing or embossing on a tangible record an official stamp

2. An electronic device or process that is capable of attaching to or association with an electronic record of an official stamp

Sufficiency

A certificate of notarial act is adequate, provided it meets the following requirements:

- It is concise or short

- It is in a form allowed by the law

- It is in a form permitted in the county/jurisdiction where the notary act is performed

Protests of a Negotiable Instrument

A protest is a certificate of dishonor made by a US

consul, vice consul, or a notary public. The protest must:

- Identify the negotiable instrument.

- Certify if the presentation has or has not been made and why

- State that the instrument is dishonored by non-payment or non-acceptance

- Notice of dishonor has to be given to some or all parties.

- The individual requesting the protest has to physically appear before the notary public and be identified.

- The notary public must know the person or have satisfactory evidence of the identity of the individual requesting the protest.

- A notary can charge up to $3 per page for noting a protest of a negotiable instrument.

Official Notary Stamp & Journal

All PA notaries must record each notarial act. This includes affixing a seal or stamp to the document. The rubber seal should show the following:

- Words- Commonwealth of PA

- Words- Notary seal

- Notary's name and the word 'Notary Public'

- Name of the county where the notary public

maintains an office

- Date when the commission expires

- The seven-digit commission ID

Official Stamp

1. If a notary act is performed on a tangible record, an official stamp has to be affixed to the certificate near the signature.

2. The stamp must be in a form that is photographically reproducible.

The following applies to the notary stamp:

All notaries need to have an official seal which shall be used to authenticate all notary acts. The rubber seal must show the following:

- Words "Commonwealth of Pennsylvania."

- Words "Notary Seal."

- Name as it appears on the commission and words

"Notary Public."

• Name of the county where the notary public maintains an office

• Date commission expires

• Seal must have a maximum height of one inch and a width of 3 and a half inches, with a plain border

• Seal must be capable of being copied after it is stamped to the document

Security of Seal

1. The notary public is responsible for the security of the seal.

2. No other individual is allowed to use the seal.

3. Upon resignation or expiration of commission, the seal can be disabled by defacing, destroying, erasing, or damaging it -making it unusable.

4. If the individual is suspended or revoked, the stamp has to be surrendered.

5. On the death of the notary public, the personal guardian shall render the seal unusable.

6. If the seal is lost or stolen, the notary public must notify the Department immediately.

Seal Dimensions

• Seal must have a maximum height of 1 inch, and maximum width of 3.5 inches, and a plain border.

• Seal must be capable of being copied.

• No words can be abbreviated on the stamp.

Legible

When using the seal, the following is important:

1. Place the stamp in a prominent location on the certificate near the signature

2. Ensure it is photographically reproducible

3. Make it legible

4. The stamp should not cover any text, print, or

signature

5. The seal should leave a clear impression

Revised Uniform Law on Stamp

• It must be kept in a secure location where only the notary public can access it

• Must be always under the control of the notary public

• It cannot be used by another individual

• Use of a notary seal by another person is a crime

• Only to be used for notarial acts

• Should not be altered or defaced

Lost or Stolen Seal

If the seal is lost or stolen, it must be reported to the Department in writing or electronically within ten days-immediately if possible. The notification should include the following:

• What happened to the stamp? Is it lost, stolen, or

misplaced?

- When was it discovered that the seal was missing?

- A statement that the notary public does not have a stamp and does not know where his stamp is located or misplaced

- Statement to say that the stamp is found; the Department should be notified within ten days

Seal Disposal or Destruction

1. If the notary commission is revoked or suspended, the stamp must be sent back to the Dept within ten days.

2. If the notary public resigns or if the commission expires, the notary public must disable the seal by destroying and rendering it unusable.

3. In case of death, the personal representative must disable the seal and make it unusable.

Embossing the Seal

1. It can be embossed if the notary public wants

2. The name and everything else must be the same as it appears on the commission.

3. Words- 'Commonwealth of Pennsylvania' must be shown

4. The words 'notary public' must be shown.

5. An embossed seal may only be used in conjunction with an official stamp. If the name is changed, the same embossed seal can be used as long as it states that the notary public commission is not expired.

6. When using the embossed seal, do not overlap any signature, official stamp, or text.

Notary Journal

1. The Notary public must maintain a journal and record in chronological order all notarial acts

2. A journal may be in a tangible medium or electronic format

3. If tangible format, all pages have to be numbered

4. If in an electronic format, it should be in temper-evident electronic format and comply with department regulations

Entries in the Journal

- It must be in a chronological manner.

- Date and time of each act

- Description of the record and notarial act

- Full name and address of each individual for whom the notarial act was done

- If the ID of an individual is based on personal knowledge, a statement is required.

- If the ID is based on satisfactory evidence, then a description of the ID, date issue, and expiration date has to be stated.

- The fee charged by the notary has to be stated.

The Journal Rules

1. The notary public has to maintain a notary journal with a chronological record of all notarial acts.

2. The notary journal may be electronic or paper-based

3. If the Journal is lost or stolen, the notary public must report it immediately to the Department.

4. If the notary resigns, there is revocation, or the commission expires, he or she must deliver the Journal to the recorder of deeds in the county within 30 days.

5. Death. If the notary public dies, then the personal representative must deliver the Journal within 30 days to the recorder of deeds in the county of practice.

Journal Protection

1. Journal and each public record are exempt from execution

2. Journal belongs to the notary public

3. The Journal cannot be used by any other person or

surrendered to the employer

Notary Journal Requirements

- Notary name as it appears on the commission

- Notary commission number

- Commission expiration date

- Office address

- A statement in the event of death that the Journal needs to be mailed or delivered to the office of the recorder of deeds

- All uncommonly abbreviated words or symbols need to be defined or not used at all.

- Names should never be abbreviated.

- The notary signature must be present on each entry.

- Edits can be made, but the date of the edit has to be recorded.

- All pages have to be numbered consecutively starting

from page 1.

Contents of Notary Journal

Notary entry must contain the following:

• Date and time of the notarial act

• Description of the document

• Type of notarial act performed.

• The name and address of each individual for whom the notarial act is performed

• Each notary act must be a separate entry.

• If satisfactory evidence is used to identify the individual, the notary officer must provide a short description of the type of ID used, including the date when it was issued and its expiration date.

• The fee charged must be recorded; if the fee is waived, it should state 'n/c' (no charge)

• All other clerical and administrative fees should be itemized.

Prohibited Information

1. Some information is prohibited from the journal entry.

2. Must not record personal financial or ID information about the client like SIN, driver's license number, or bank account number

Surrender of Journal

1. The notary journal is personal and should never be given to anyone. The notary public may be disqualified, resigned, removed from office, or died- in all cases, the Journal cannot be given to any other person.

2. The notary journal should not be given to any person, including the employer, even if it was paid by the company.

3. The notary public must give a certified copy of any pages of the Journal to any client who asks for it within ten days of the request.

4. The notary public may charge a fee for copying and mailing but should let the requestor know in advance of

the cost.

5. If the notary journal is stolen, lost, or damaged, the notary public must inform the Dept within ten days; the statement should include the following:

• Where the Journal was lost or stolen

• How did the Journal get lost or stolen

• Date when the notary public discovered the Journal was stolen or lost

• A statement saying that the notary does not possess the Journal and has no idea who has it

• A statement saying that if the notary public does find the Journal, he will notify the Dept within ten days

If the notary public resigns or the commission is revoked or expires, he/she must deliver the Journal within 30 days to the recorder of deeds in the county where he has an office.

If the notary public dies, then a trustworthy individual must deliver the notary journal to the office of the recorder of deeds within 30 days.

Fees & Schedule

Notary Public Fees and Notary Fee Schedule

- Fees fixed by Department

- The notary public cannot charge more fees than those set by the Department

- The notary public must state or display fees for clients

- Provide a list of fees to the client on request

- Has the right to wave a fee

- The fee belongs to the notary and not the employer

- There is no fee splitting

Caution about Fees

1. Notary fees are determined by the State, and there is a cap on fees.

2. A notary public is not allowed to charge more than the set fees.

3. Notary fees may be lower but never higher than the set amount.

4. If the notary public does not charge fees, there is no obligation to post fees.

5. A notary public may charge administrative and clerical fees for postage, copying, and telephone calls, but they have to be reasonable.

6. A notary public must inform the client of the amount of fees before performing the service.

7. An itemized receipt for all fees is a must.

Fee Schedule

1. Taking an acknowledgment - $5

2. Taking acknowledgment with each additional name - $2

3. Administering oath or affirmation - $5

4. Taking verification on oath or affirmation - $5

5. Witnessing or attesting a signature - $5

6. Certifying or attesting a copy or deposition - $5

7. Notifying a protest per page - $3

Electronic Notarization

PA Electronic Notarization

1. Electronic refers to technology that includes digital, electrical, wireless, magnetic, electromagnetic, optical, etc.

2. An electronic signature is an electronic sound or symbol attached or associated with a record and executed by an individual with the intent to sign

3. One can apply for approval to notarize electronically

after one becomes commissioned.

4. Electronic documents include email messages, pdf files, images, online documents, etc.

5. The notary will digitally place his or her identifying information on the document, which is electronic.

6. All steps for electronic notarization, including proper ID and personal appearance, must take place as if one were notarizing a paper-based document in person.

7. A notary public who wishes to perform electronic notary acts must first be an active notary commissioner and must be authorized by the Department as an e-notary public.

Selection of Technology for Electronic Notarial Acts

1. The notary public has to select a tamper-proof technology to perform electronic notarial acts.

2. The notary public can only perform electronic notarial acts with approved technology.

3. Before performing electronic notarial acts, the notary has to notify the Department and identify the different technology.

4. The chosen technology must comply with department standards.

To become an e-notary public, the Department must be provided with the following details:

- Name of the notary public

- Notary commission number

- Email address

- Office address

- Name and contact information for the electronic notarization solution provider-the website address must be provided

Making Changes to Your Commission

Name Change

1. Use the old name until the commission expires and then reapply with the new name.

2. Use a new name right away, but you will need to first register the new signature with the prothonotary and purchase a new official stamp.

3. The notary officer has to report any change in the

name to the Department and recorder of deeds in the county of practice within 30 days.

Protocol for a Name Change

1. Complete the Department form for name change and submit a photocopy to the Secretary of the Commonwealth along with evidence of name change.

2. Take the original form to a notary with an acknowledgment and have the acknowledgment completed. Remember, a notary public cannot notarize their own signature.

3. Take or mail the state form and notarized acknowledgment together with the recording fee to the recorder of deeds in the county where the office is located.

4. If using the new name, register with a new signature with the prothonotary in the county where the office is located.

Change of Address

1. Complete the Dept of State Change of address form.

2. Give a photocopy to the Secretary of the state within 30 days.

3. Purchase a new stamp if the office is in a different county.

4. If the office is moved to a different county, record the signature with the prothonotary of the new county within 30 days of change.

5. Also, send a notice to the recorder of deeds in the county of your original appointment indicating your new address.

Moving Outside of PA

1. One can move outside of PA and can continue to work as a notary public as long as one has a work address in PA.

2. If the notary public does not work or live in Pa, the notary must resign.

3. The resignation form has to be submitted to the Secretary of the Commonwealth along with the notary journal that must be sent to the recorder of deeds in the

county where the office is located.

4. All this must be done within 30 days.

5. The official notary stamp must be destroyed.

Client Identification

Recognizing the Client

During a notarial act, the client has to physically appear in front of the notary.

What is not considered valid personal appearance:

- Use of audio technology

- Video conference call

- Receive a fax to be notarized

- Receive a telephone call from the customer

- Sending another individual to have the document notarized

Personal Knowledge

A notary officer should have some personal information about the identity of the individual appearing before him if the individual is personally known.

Satisfactory Evidence

Examples include:

1. A passport that is current and not expired

2. State driving license, which is current and not expired

3. Govt issued non-driver's ID

4. Any other govt ID with a photograph

5. The verification on oath or affirmation of a credible witness who is physically present in front of the notary

officer and known to the officer

Authority to Refuse Notarial Acts

1. A notary officer can refuse to perform a notary act if he or she is not satisfied that the person appearing before him may not be competent or understands the situation. Any doubt in the mental status of the individual can lead to a refusal.

2. If the client's signature is not voluntarily made

3. If the individual is not cognitively aware or is of a sound mind

4. The individual's signature on record must confirm the signature on the ID.

Who Can Perform Notarial Acts?

Notarial acts in PA can be performed by any of the following:

• Judge of court

• A pronotary, clerk, or deputy clerk of the court

having a seal

- A recorder of deeds

- A deputy recorder of deeds

- A notary public

- A member of the minor judiciary

- Any individual authorized by law to perform a specific notarial act

Notarial Act in Another State

A notarial act can be performed in another state, and it has the same legal binding as if it was done under Pennsylvania law by a notary officer of the commonwealth as long as the following criteria are met:

- Must be a notary public of that state

- Can be a clerk, judge, or deputy clerk of that state

- Any individual authorized by law to perform notarial acts

- Prima facie evidence that the signature and title of the individual performing the notarial act are genuine

Indian Tribe

Notarial acts under the authority of federally recognized Indian tribes.

A notarial act performed under the authority and in a federally recognized Indian tribe has the same effect as if performed anywhere else in the commonwealth as long as it meets the following

- A notary public of the tribe

- A judge, clerk, or deputy of a court of the tribe

- An individual authorized by the law of the tribe to perform a notarial act

- There is prima facie evidence that the signature and title of the person performing the notarial act are genuine

Notarial Act Under Federal Authority

A notarial act under Federal law has the same effect as if it is performed by a notary from the commonwealth as long as the:

- It is a judge clerk or deputy of the court

- An individual in military service under military authority and authorized to perform notary acts

- An individual designated an NP by the US state department

- An individual authorized by federal law

- There is prima facie evidence that the individual under federal authority has a valid title and signature is genuine

Legal Matters

RULONA or Revised Uniform Law on Notarial Acts. RULONA was first created by a non-governmental entity called the Uniform Law Commission. This entity was formed to ensure that the laws were standardized for commerce and business across the United States. RULONA promotes uniformity in Notary Laws and ensures that the administrative rules in the different states are similar. RULONA has addressed the issue of electronic notarization, and the law has been adopted in Nevada, Iowa, North Dakota, Montana, West Virginia and Pennsylvania.

Convictions

Irrespective of whether a judgment has been rendered, the applicant needs to state the entire past legal history. It should include the following:

• Entry of plea of guilt or nolo contendere

• A guilty verdict

• A not guilty verdict as a result of a mental illness or insanity

Conflicts of Interest

A notary office should not perform a notarial act if the spouse has a direct financial interest.

None of the below constitute a conflict of interest.

• If the individual is a shareholder in a publicly traded corporation that regularly conducts notarized transactions

• Being an officer, employee, or CEO of a corporation that regularly conducts notarized transactions unless the individual performing the notarization personally gains from the endeavor.

Immunity

1. The notary public must act in an appropriate manner during the term of the commission

2. There is no immunity or benefit conferred on public officials or employees

Sanctions

The Department has complete authority to deny, refuse, revoke, suspend, or reprimand a notary public for an act or omission which reflects that the candidate lacks integrity, honesty, competence, and reliability. Such acts include the following:

• Failure to comply with rules

• Dishonest or fraudulent misstatement or commission in application

- A conviction for a felony or an offense involving dishonesty, fraud, or deceit

- A finding against or admission of liability or disciplinary action based on dishonesty, fraud, or deceit

- Use of misleading or false advertising

- Violation of regulations set by the Department

- Denial, refusal to renew, revocation, or suspension of commission in another state

- Failure to maintain the bond

Administrative Penalty

1. The Department can impose a penalty of $1,000 for each act or omission which is considered a violation during the performance of a notarial act.

2. The client may also seek civil or criminal remedies as provided by law.

Investigations

1. The Dept may issue a subpoena if there are disciplinary issues or violations of the provisions of the law.

2. During the investigations, the Dept may administer oaths, examine a witness, and take testimony.

Criminal penalties may apply when:

• One individual pretends to act as a notary public or performs a notarial act when not commissioned

• Use of the official stamp by a non-notary public

• This can result in a fine of not more than $1,000

Database of Notary Public Officers

The Department does maintain an electronic database of notary public officers in the State. This data is collected from the applications and those who register to practice electronically.

Prohibited Acts

1. The Notary public does not have authority in legal matters

2. Cannot act as an immigration consult

3. Cannot represent a person in judicial matters

4. Cannot receive compensation for the above matters

False Advertising

1. Cannot engage in false or deceptive advertising

2. Cannot use the words 'notario' or 'notario publico' when placing an ad.

3. If a notary public does advertise, he or she should add a disclaimer that he is not a lawyer and cannot give advice on legal matters.

Regulations

• Prescribe the notarial acts according to the rules and regulations established by the Commonwealth of PA.

• Include provisions to ensure any change or tampering with a record-bearing certificate is self-evident.

• Include provisions to ensure integrity in the creation, transmittal, storage, and authentication of electronic records or signatures.

Examination and Education

The Basic Public Education Course

• All applicants must pass the exam administered by the Commonwealth.

• Basic education; all applicants must, within six months of preceding application must, complete a three-hour course of notary basic public education.

• This course covers statutes, procedures, regulations,

and ethics of relevance to the notary public.

- The course can be either interactive or classroom-based

Continuing Education

- For renewal of the commission, a notary must complete within six months preceding the application a 3-hour public continuing education course.

- The course can be interactive or classroom-based

- All courses need to be pre-approved by the Department.

Exam

1. Only those individuals approved by the State are allowed to schedule the exam. The application for the exam can be done electronically.

2. It takes about four weeks for the review of the application and approval

3. If the application is approved, a notice to register for

the exam is sent to the applicant.

4. The fee for the exam is $65 and is not refundable.

5. The Commonwealth of PA does allow for online testing, but each candidate is only given one opportunity to take the Notary exam. If the candidate fails the online exam, he or she has to register at a physical testing site to take the exam.

Exam Content

1. The exam consists of 25 scored and five pretest multiple-choice questions with only one correct answer. Each question will have three answer options.

2. The duration of the exam is 60 minutes.

3. There should be no attempt to cheat. Otherwise, you will be immediately asked to leave the exam hall. In addition, no exam material can be removed from the room- or you face legal charges.

4. Soon after the exam, preliminary results are provided. A passing score of 75 is required.

Glossary Terms

Acknowledgment is a formal declaration before a notarial officer by an individual signing an instrument that such execution is an independent act/deed- free from any duress or coercion.

Administer is a process where the notary public performs the duties of an office; for example, giving an oath.

An affidavit is a document with written facts made voluntarily and confirmed by the oath or affirmation of the party made in front of an individual authorized to administer oaths, i.e., a notary public. The term includes an oath or affirmation.

Affirm is where one makes a formal, solemn declaration under the penalty of perjury that the statements one is making are not false.

Affirmation is legally equivalent to an oath; it is sometimes used as an alternative to an oath. Essentially the individual states that he or she will tell the truth.

Affix is the process where one impresses or attaches the notary seal to an instrument.

Apostille is a certificate of notarial authority that is issued by the Dept of Foreign Affairs or Secretary of the Commonwealth. Apostille usually applies to marriage certificates, degrees and diplomas that need to be certified for use abroad.

Attest is the process where one bears witness to or certifies.

Attorney In Fact is the individual who has been authorized to act for another attorney by a power of attorney.

Authentication is the process or action that proves something to be genuine, true, or valid. An apostille certificate is often authenticated by the Dept of Foreign Affairs.

A Bill of sale is a written document that is given from the vendor to the vendee.

A certified copy is a copy of a document certified as a true copy by the notary public- who usually has custody of the original document. When a notary makes a certified copy, he/she determines that the photocopy is a complete and accurate reproduction of an original document that was presented to him/her. A notary cannot guarantee the authenticity of the original document or its contents.

Codicil is an instrument created subsequent to a will and attached to the original will when some edits are required.

The commission is the term used to denote the duration of the appointment as a notary public by the Secretary of the Commonwealth.

A contract is a legal agreement between competent parties. It is usually in writing and clearly states what rights each party has.

The custodian of the document is the individual who has custody or charge of the document. The custodian is usually the individual who presents the document or paper. However, when making an attested photocopy, the custodian of the document may or may not be the person who signed the document.

A deed is a legal document that conveys the transfer of real estate property.

A Deponent is a person who takes an oath confirming that the written statement is true.

A deposition is a process where the testimony of a witness is taken out of court under oath or by affirmation before a lawyer or a notary public. The testimony authorized by law can be used at a trial or a hearing.

Discretion: Sometimes, the notary public may behave in a discrete manner. When using discretion, the individual will speak or behave in such a way as to avoid creating any friction, outbursts or revealing confidential information.

An electronic notarial act is an official and legal act performed by a notary public who is physically present in Pennsylvania. It may also involve maintaining an electronic record and only using communication technology that has been authorized.

An electronic notary public officer is someone who has registered with the Secretary of State and wants to participate in electronic notarization. However, he or she first has to show that the devices that will be used comply with the State rules.

Electronic record -information that is generated, created, communicated, sent, received, and stored by electronic means.

An electronic signature is any electronic signature affixed to an electronic notary in the performance of an electronic notarial act.

Execute a document: to perform all the necessary tasks needed to make the instrument or document fully effective. In general, when executing a document, this also refers to signing the document.

A felony is a much more serious crime than a

misdemeanor and is frequently punished by prolonged incarceration or even death.

Free act and deed are where one admits what one has done and assumes responsibility for the outcome.

Grantee is the individual who becomes the recipient of the deed of the real estate property.

Grantor (usually the seller) is the individual who transfers the deed of the real estate property to the grantee.

Identity verification- use of an authentic process by which a notary validates the identity of the principal and other individuals present for the notarial act

An instrument is essentially a written document.

A lease is a contract where one obtains possession or control of a property/motor vehicle for a defined amount of time.

Lessee is the individual or family who rents the real estate property from another party.

Lessor is usually the person who rents the real estate property to the lessee.

Lien is a right or a legal claim to a specific real estate property. The lien is released when the debt is paid.

Litigation is the act of bringing about a lawsuit.

Malfeasance is an act that one should not be doing-usually a crime.

A misdemeanor is any other crime other than a felony.

Misfeasance is an illegal or improper act that a lawful individual may do.

Negligence is the failure to use due and reasonable care that a normal person would use under similar circumstances.

A notarial act is one that can be performed with respect to an electronic or tangible record- the act is usually performed by a notary public commissioned in the Commonwealth of PA. There are 6 types of notarial acts that the notary officer will commonly perform.

A notary certificate is a written statement made by the notary public. This document will certify certain facts of the notarial act that was performed.

A notary public is an individual who meets the qualifications and is appointed by the Secretary of State to perform the six notarial acts under RULONA.

An oath is any form of pledge or attestation through which an individual signifies that he or she is morally and ethically bound to a supreme being to state an honest and truthful statement. Intentionally swearing and making untrue statements constitute a charge of perjury.

An official stamp is a physical image afield or embossed on a tangible record on an electronic image attached to an electronic record. The term will include a notary seal.

Perjury is intentionally making a false statement under oath or affirmation. Perjury is a crime that is considered a felony and punishable with a monetary fine and/or incarceration.

Personal appearance means presence at a translation for which a notarial act is required, either electronically or physically, in a manner that meets all requirements.

A plaintiff is an individual who initiates a lawsuit against another individual.

Power of attorney is a written statement by a person giving another individual the power to act on his or her behalf.

The principal is the individual who makes a power of attorney.

The proof is defined as a formal declaration that is usually made by a subscribing witness when executing an instrument. The witness usually states that he knows the individual described in the instrument and saw him execute the instrument.

Protest Is a formal statement written by the notary under seal that a certain payment or promissory note was presented and that such payment was refused.

Principal refers to the individual whose signature is reflected on a record that is notarized and 2) who has taken an oath or affirmation administered by the notary.

A quitclaim deed is a document where the grantor disclaims all interest in a real estate property and then conveys that interest to a grantee. Unlike other deeds, the quitclaim grantor does not promise that his or her interest in the property is actually valid.

Reasonable care is defined as the degree of care which an individual of ordinary intelligence and prudence would exercise when faced with the same or similar situation. When one fails to exercise reasonable care, this is known as negligence.

A recorder of deeds is an official or county recorder of deeds. The term may include the commissioner of records and manager of the dept of real estate of a county of the second class.

Satisfactory evidence- A notary public officer needs to identify the person appearing before him. Some of the IDs that can be used to identify the individual include a passport, driver's license, and government-issued photo ID- all IDs need to be current and have the signature of the individual. The notary public can also perform verification on oath or affirmation of the credible witness who is personally known to the officer.

Seal is required by all notaries. The seal should identify the notary public, the jurisdiction of practice, and the authority.

Signature of notary: All notaries must sign their name; in addition, the notary must print or stamp beneath his signature in ink his name, the name of the county where qualified, and the date when the commission expires.

Statue: Law established by an act of the legislature.

Subscribe means signing of an instrument.

Swear means one takes an oath.

Taking an acknowledgment is an act of the individual named in the instrument who tells the notary that he is the individual named in the instrument and acknowledges that he executed the instrument. At the same time, this also involves the notary public obtaining satisfactory evidence of the person's identity.

Venue: Geographical place where the notary public takes the acknowledgment or affidavit. Venue must be listed on all notarized documents.

Practice Test #1

1. How long is the term of commission for a notary public in PA?

a. Two years

b. Three years

c. Four years

d. Five years

Answer C

The Notary commission for officers lasts four years. A renewal is required every four years.

2. If a notary public suddenly dies, the personal representative must deliver the journal to the Recorder of Deeds within what time period?

a. Seven days

b. Ten days

c. 15 days

d. 30 days

Answer D

If the notary public dies, the personal representative or guardian who has knowledge about the journal should deliver it to the Recorder of deeds in the county where the Notary had his practice. The journal should preferably be delivered within 30 days after the death.

3. What is the fee for noting a protest of a negotiable instrument?

a. $3

b. $4

c. $5

d. $7

Answer A

The fee for noting a protest of a negotiable instrument (per page) is $3

4. The Notary public fees are set by the:

a. County clerk

b. Department of State

c. The Recorder of deeds

d. The State auditor

Answer B

Notary fees are set by the Department of State. Notaries may charge lower fees but cannot charge more than the specified amount.

5. What is the minimum age requirement to become a notary public in PA?

a. 16

b. 18

c. 20

d. 22

Answer B

The minimum age an applicant has to be when applying for a notary commission in PA is 18 years of age.

6. To become a notary public in PA, the applicant may be all of the following EXCEPT?

a. American Citizen

b. Permanent legal resident

c. A resident of Pennsylvania

d. Undocumented immigrant

Answer D

In general, illegals and undocumented immigrants cannot apply to be a notary public in the Commonwealth. One can be a US citizen or a permanent legal resident.

7. To be appointed as a notary public in the Commonwealth, the notary public may?

a. Have a business office in the state

b. Remotely work from another state

c. Work from outside the state as long as he visits PA once a year

d. Work out of state by obtaining permission from the Secretary

Answer A

To work as a notary public in PA, one either has to be a resident or have a business office in the Commonwealth.

8. What is the fee for taking an acknowledgment in the Commonwealth?

a. $3

b. $5

c. $7

d. $10

Answer B

The Notary public fee for taking an acknowledgment is $5

9. What is the fee for taking an acknowledgment with each additional name?

a. $2

b. $3

c. $4

d. $5

Answer A

For each additional name added to the acknowledgment, the fee is $2.

10. In order to be commissioned as a notary public in PA, the individual should be able to read and write what language(s)?

a. English

b. Spanish

c. Both English and Spanish

d. English and Amish

Answer A

All applicants for the notary commission job must be able to read and write English.

11. Once commissioned as a notary public officer, the candidate must obtain a surety bond in what amount?

a. $2,000

b. $5,000

c. $7,500

d. $10,000

Answer D

The notary public officer needs to obtain a surety bond from a private insurer for $10,000. This is not an insurance policy, and the money needs to be paid back if there are any claims against the notary officer.

12. Within what time period after appointment a notary public must obtain a surety bond?

a. Seven days

b. Fifteen days

c. 30 days

d. 45 days

Answer D

Once the notary public has been commissioned, he or she needs to obtain a surety bond within 45 days in order to practice.

13. If a notary public moves to practice in a different county in the Commonwealth, within what time period must his or her official signature be registered?

a. Seven days

b. 14 days

c. 30 days

d. 45 days

Answer C

After moving to a new county, the official signature must be registered within 30 days.

14. Where should the notary public officer register his/her signature in a county of the second class?

a. Secretary of state

b. Mayor's office

c. Clerk of courts

d. Judge

Answer C

In a county of second class, the signature of the notary public has to be registered with the clerk of the Courts.

15. Within how many days after the appointment as a notary public should the individual obtain a surety bond?

a. Seven days

b. Fifteen days

c. 30 days

d. 45 days

Answer D

Once appointed as a notary public officer but before a commission is issued, the Notary must obtain a surety bond within 45 days.

16. A notary public cannot issue a certified copy of?

a. College transcript

b. Driver's license

c. A Bill of sale

d. A birth certificate

Answer D

A notary cannot issue a certified copy of a death or

birth certificate.

17. Which of the following data can be added to the notary journal?

a. The client's social security number

b. The client's driver's license number

c. The client's credit card number

d. The fee for the service

Answer D

There are a few items that cannot be added to the notary journal, and they include personal and financial data. The fee for the notarial act must be added to the journal.

18. Which of the following terms does not appear on the notary seal?

a. The words ' Commonwealth of Pennsylvania'

b. The words 'notary public'

c. The commission expiration date

d. The address of the notary public

Answer D

The address of the notary public is not listed on the seal, but the name of the county of practice where the Notary maintains an office is.

19. What is the fee for noting a protest of a negotiable instrument?

a. $1

b. $2

c. $3

d. $4

Answer C

The fee for noting a protest of a negotiable instrument is $3.00

20. In the Commonwealth of Pennsylvania, is a Notary public able to waive fees for notarial acts?

a. No

b. Yes

c. It depends on the type of notarial act

d. Has to get permission from the state department first

Answer B

A notary public does not have to charge fees for the services. The choice to waive fees is personal.

Practice Test #2

1. What fee is the notary public allowed to charge for witnessing a signature?

a. $2

b. $3

c. $4

d. $5

Answer D

The fee for witnessing or attesting a signature is $5.00

2. What is the fee for certifying a copy of a deposition?

a. $2

b. $3

c. $4

d. $5

Answer D

The fee for certifying or attesting a copy or deposition is $5.00

3. In the Commonwealth of Pennsylvania, what is the fee for taking an acknowledgment by a Notary public?

a. $2

b. $3

c. $4

d. $5

Answer D

The fee for taking an acknowledgment is $5.00

4. What is the fee when taking an acknowledgment

with each additional name?

a. $1

b. $2

c. $3

d. $4

Answer B

The fee for taking an acknowledgment each additional name is $2.00

5. What is the fee to register the official signature of a notary public with the prothonotary's office?

a. $0.50

b. $2

c. $3

d. $4

Answer A

To register the official signature with the prothonotary's office, the fee is $0.50. The Notary must practice in the county where the official signature is registered.

6. Following a reappointment as a notary public, within what time must the individual register the official signature?

a. Seven days

b. Fourteen days

c. 30 days

d. 45 days

Answer D

Following a new appointment or reappointment, the official signature of the notary public must be registered within 45 days in the county where the business is established.

7. If the Notary public moves to practice in a different county, he or she should register their official signature within how many days?

a. Seven days

b. 14 days

c. 21 days

d. 30 days

Answer D

If the Notary public changes practice to a different county, the official signature must be registered within 30 days.

8. After recording the bond, oath of office, and commission with the office of the Recorder of deeds, within what time frame should a copy of the bond and

oath of office be filed with the Department?

a. 15 days

b. 30 days

c. 60 days

d. 90 days

Answer D

A copy of the bond and oath of office must be filed with the Department within 90 days.

9. Sometimes, the surety or issuing entity may cancel the notary bond. How many days' notice should it provide to the Department before the cancellation?

a. Seven days

b. 14 days

c. 21 days

d. 30 days

Answer D

Sometimes the surety or issuing entity wants to cancel the bond. They have to give the Department at least 30 days' notice before the notary bond can be canceled.

10. The law states that all recordings in the notary journal should be:

a. In black ink

b. In a chronological fashion

c. Recorded in an alphabetical manner

d. Written in small paragraphs

Answer B

The rules for recording in the notary journal state that everything should be documented in chronological order.

11. A paper-bound journal should always be?

a. Made into a photocopy

b. Numbered

c. In blue ink

d. Carried at all times with the notary public

Answer B

If the notary public decides to have a paper-based notary journal, all the pages must be consecutively numbered.

12. In the event there is the sudden death of a notary public, the personal representative shall deliver the notary journal to whom?

a. Secretary of state

b. Prothonotary

c. Recorder of deeds

d. The attorney

Answer C

If the notary public were to die, then the personal representative should deliver the notary journal to the Recorder of deeds. The journal can be hand delivered or mailed.

13. In the event of a death of a notary public, the personal representative shall deliver the notary journal to the office of the Recorder of deeds within what time?

a. Seven days

b. 14 days

c. 21 days

d. 30 days

Answer D

If the notary public were to die, then the personal representative should deliver the notary journal to the

Recorder of deeds. The journal can be hand delivered or mailed; this should be done within 30 days.

14. Each notarial act in the Commonwealth of Pennsylvania will have evidence of a?

a. Certificate

b. Paid invoice

c. Stamp

d. Photocopy

Answer A

A notarial certificate is always executed when performing a notarial act.

15. A notary public forgets to give a bond and fails to record the oath and commission. This inactivity can lead to a null commission within how many days?

a. Seven days

b. 15 days

c. 21 days

d. 45 days

Answer D

If the notary public fails to file the oath and commission and fails to give a bond, his or her commission will be void in 45 days.

16. During reappointment as a notary public, where or with whom should the individual record the notary bond, oath of office as well as commission?

a. Office of the Recorder of deeds

b. Secretary of State

c. Prothonotary's office

d. Lawyer

Answer A

The Notary must record the bond, oath of office, and commission with the office of the Recorder of deeds. This should be done in the county where the Notary retains the business office.

17. In general, for reappointment as a notary public in the Commonwealth, the individual should file an application how long before the term expires?

a. 12 months

b. Nine months

c. Six months

d. Two months

Answer D

In general, for reappointments, the Notary should reapply two months before the commission actually expires. Failure to do so may mean retaking the notary exam all over again.

18. Which of the following notarial acts can the notary public in the Commonwealth not do?

a. Administer an oath

b. Take an affidavit

c. Witness a signature

d. Depose the plaintiff

Answer D

In general, anything to do with the law is forbidden. A Notary public is not permitted to depose any individual.

19. An acknowledgment can be taken within the Commonwealth of Pennsylvania by:

a. Deputy of any federal court

b. Mayor

c. Member of US congress

d. A criminal court Judge

Answer A

An acknowledgment of any instrument can be taken within the Commonwealth by a US clerk or deputy of any federal court. The rest of the individuals mentioned are not permitted to do so.

20. When entering the names of a client in the journal following a notarial act, what terms should the Notary public use?

a. Abbreviations if the client also uses them

b. Full name at all times

c. Depends on what the client prefers

d. Nickname

Answer B

At all times, when performing notarial acts and recording in the journal, the client's proper name in full should be used. Abbreviations are not permitted.

Practice Test #3

1. Which of the following is not an approved notarial act by the Department?

a. Taking a verification on oath

b. Attesting a signature

c. Certifying a marriage

d. Noting a protest of a negotiable instrument

Answer C

A notary public in the Commonwealth cannot certify a marriage. This can only be done by people who have been appointed by the Clergy or people who have been registered with the Registrar General.

2. All applicants for the notary public commission in the Commonwealth are required to take the public basic education course. What is the duration of this course?

a. 1 hour

b. 2 hours

c. 3 hours

d. 6 hours

Answer C

The public basic education course that is required of all applicants is 3 hours long and has to be approved by the Department. The applicant must show evidence that the course was taken when applying for a notary public officer.

3. Can a Notary public waive a fee for an acknowledgment?

a. Yes

b. No

c. Only for relatives

d. Only for government employees

Answer A

The notary public is at liberty to waive fees. There is no rule that says that fees cannot be waived.

4. In general, the fees for notarial services are the property of?

a. Employer

b. Notary public

c. Workers who share the office

d. Notary public and employer

Answer B

The notary fees belong to the notary public. They should not be shared- not even with the employer unless there is a prior contract.

5. If a notary wants to charge administrative and clerical fees, he or she should first inform:

a. The state Department

b. The client

c. The county Clerk

d. The Secretary

Answer B

A notary public can charge clerical and administrative fees, but first, he or she should always inform the client about these extra costs. As long as the fees are reasonable, they are allowed.

6. When a notary public violates provisions set by RULONA, what type of sanctions may be imposed?

a. Suspension of the commission

b. Refusal to renew the commission

c. Reprimand

d. All of the above

Answer D

When a notary public violates the rules set by
RULONA, the sanctions may include denial, refusal to
renew, suspension, and reprimand, or the Department
may impose a restrictive condition on a commission as a
notary public.

7. If a notary public no longer resides in the
Commonwealth or has a business office, within what time
should he notify the Department regarding his
resignation?

a. Seven days

b. 15 days

c. 21 days

d. 30 days

Answer D

If the notary public no longer has a business in the Commonwealth and now resides out of state, he or she should notify the Department of the resignation within 30 days. Working as a notary public in such circumstances is a crime.

8. If the notary public loses his stamping device, within what time must he notify the Department in writing or electronically?

a. Three days

b. Five days

c. Seven days

d. Ten days

Answer D

If the stamping device is lost or misplaced, the notary public must notify the Department within ten days, either by writing or electronically. A personal representative can also notify the Department if the notary public is not able to do so.

9. In general, when creating a journal of a notarial act, what information should not be added?

a. Client's social security number

b. Date and time of the notarial act

c. Name of the client

d. Type of notarial act performed

Answer A

When recording in the notary journal, the notary officer should avoid all personal and financial information of the client. The social security number, driver's license number or numbers of credit cards should not be recorded in the journal.

10. A notary public decides to waive the fee for a notarial act. What should he record in the journal?

a. No need to document if there is no fee

b. Write 'n/c' in the journal

c. Explain why the fee was waived

Answer B

When a fee for a notary act is waived, it still needs to be recorded in the journal. The Notary can simply write 'n/c', meaning no charge.

11. Within what time preceding the application for a notary public commission should the applicant complete the public basic education course?

a. 15 days

b. Two months

c. Three months

d. Six months

Answer D

The applicant should complete the public basic education course within six months preceding the application. The course to be taken must be approved by the Department.

12. If the insurer wants to cancel the bond, within what time must the surety issuing entity notify the Department before canceling the bond?

a. Seven days

b. 15 days

c. 21 days

d. 30 days

Answer D

In general, if the surety issuing entity wants to cancel the bond for the notary public, it must give a 30-day notice before cancellation.

13. A notary public's signature on an acknowledgment is not legible. What is the next step?

a. Not worry about it

b. Ask a colleague to sign for him

c. Print his name next to the signature

d. Erase the signature and apply a seal

Answer C

If the notary officer's signature is not recognizable or legible, he or she should legibly print the full name just next to the signature.

14. When attaching a notarial certificate to a tangible record, what method can be used to secure the document?

a. Staples

b. Tape

c. Binder clips

d. Paper clips

Answer A

When attaching a notarial certificate to a tangible record, one should use staples. Tape and paper clips are not secure enough.

15. Which one of the following does not satisfy the requirements for performing an electronic notarial act?

a. Video appearance of the individual

b. Identification of the individual

c. Use of an official seal

d. Completion of the notarial certificate

Answer A

The physical appearance of the client is necessary for all notarial acts. The notary public should not rely on video or digital images as substitutes.

16. What requirement is different for an electronic notarization compared to the conventional tangible notarial act?

a. They both have the same requirements for completing a notarial act

b. Electronic notarization does not require the physical presence of the client

c. The electronic process does not require a seal

d. Only the tangible record needs to be documented in the notary journal

Answer A

In general, the requirements for performing a notarial act via electronic means or a tangible paper-based method are the same. Both require the physical presence and identification of the client, completion of the notarial certificate, recording in the journal, and use of an official stamp.

17. If a client requires certification of documents for overseas use, he or she should contact the?

a. Notary public

b. Secretary

c. US Dept of State

d. The recorder of deeds

Answer C

Certifying certain documents for overseas use is done by the State Department, Ministry of Foreign affairs, or consular services. Examples include a degree or college diploma, corporate documents, and marriage records.

18. A Notary public is not permitted to do which of the

following in the Commonwealth?

a. Oaths and affirmations

b. Verification on oaths and affirmations

c. Acknowledgments

d. Certify immigration papers

Answer D

In general, a notary public cannot assume any duties that pertain to law, and this includes certifying immigration papers.

19. As a notary public in the Commonwealth, you can?

a. Offer basic legal advice

b. Notarize your own signature

c. Ask that all clients physically show up for the notary act

d. Talk about immigration matters with clients

Answer C

As a notary public, one cannot talk about legal matters or even offer an opinion on legal matters like immigration. However, for all notarial acts, the client has to physically show up and have proper identification.

20. What is false about acceptable identification for a notarial process in the Commonwealth?

a. The ID must contain a photograph

b. The ID should contain a signature

c. The ID should not be expired for more than five years

d. A current driver's license is a valid ID

Answer C

In order for an ID to be valid for use in the Commonwealth, it has to be current and not expired. Any expired ID cannot be used for identification purposes.

Practice Test #4

1. When a notary public asks for an ID from a client, what is one major requirement?

a. It should be a colored photograph only

b. It can only be a government-issued ID

c. It must have a photograph

d. It can be an expired passport

Answer C

No matter what ID is used, it must have a photograph. Hence any ID with a photograph can be used, provided it is from a bona fide entity.

2. What are the two key requirements that the notary public should follow for any notarial act?

a. The person be physically present and clean-shaven

b. The person be physically present and have a photo ID

c. The person is physically present and speaks English

d. The person be physically present and be at least age 18

Answer B

To complete a notarial act, the client has to be physically present and have a photo Id.

3. When an individual has a history of falsifying official papers, his or her chances of becoming a notary public in the Commonwealth are?

a. Low

b. Average

c. Nil

d. Depends on the seriousness of the crime

Answer C

In general, any individual who has been charged with falsifying official papers or committing perjury has no chance of becoming a notary public in the Commonwealth.

4. To pass the Pennsylvania notary exam, one needs to obtain a score of at least?

a. 60

b. 65

c. 70

d. 75

Answer D

To pass the Pennsylvania notary exam, the candidate must have a score of at least 75.

5. An applicant for a notary public commission in the

Commonwealth is required to take a state-approved basic education course that is of what duration?

a. 1 hour

b. 2 hours

c. 3 hours

d. 6 hours

Answer C

The basic public education course is required of all applicants. The course has a minimum duration of 3 hours and has to be state approved.

6. If a notary public wishes to perform electronic notarial acts, he must first be authorized by the following:

a. Vendor

b. County clerk

c. Department

d. Internet provider

Answer C

Any notary public who wishes to perform electronic notarization must first get approval from the State. The notary public has to show evidence that the electronic means that will be used are safe, secure, and comply with the Department's requirements.

7. What are the general rules for the use of nicknames during a notarial act?

a. Not permitted

b. Only permitted if the nickname is defined

c. It can only be used for close friends

d. Can only be used after obtaining permission from the client

Answer A

No nicknames, initials, or abbreviations are acceptable for use either on the application or during the performance of notarial acts. The full name of the client must be stated.

8. Prior to applying for a notary public position, the individual has to take a basic education course. After completion of this course, how long is the certificate valid from the date of issue?

a. One month

b. Three months

c. Six months

d. 12 months

Answer C

The basic public education certificate is valid for six months from the date of issue.

9. What should be the maximum height of the notary seal?

a. 0.5 inches

b. 1 inch

c. 1.5 inches

Answer B

The notary seal should have a maximum height of 1 inch.

10. What should be the maximum diameter of the notary seal?

a. 2 inches

b. 2.5 inches

c. 3 inches

d. 3.5 inches

Answer D

The maximum diameter of the notary seal should be

3.5 inches.

11. Within how many days must a notary public register his signature if he moves from Erie county to Allegheny county?

a. Seven days

b. Fourteen days

c. 21 days

d. 30 days

Answer D

When moving to a new county, the notary public should register his signature within 30 days.

12. The Revised Uniform Law on Notarial Acts is also known as?

a. RULONA

b. Act of the Commonwealth

c. Official Notary Act

d. RULE

Answer A

The Revised Uniform Law on Notarial Acts is abbreviated as RULONA

13. What is the term called when an individual makes a declaration in front of a notary that he is the individual who signed the document and did so voluntarily?

a. Oath

b. Affirmation

c. Acknowledgement

d. Promise

Answer C

An acknowledgment is a declaration made in front of a notary that the individual who signed the document is the person appearing before him and signed the document voluntarily.

14. A notary public recently has had some changes in his business practice. Within what time should he notify the Department about these changes?

a. Seven days

b. 14 days

c. 21 days

d. 30 days

Answer D

If there are any changes related to the practice of a notary, the individual must inform the Department within 30 days of these changes.

15. Within what time period after recording the bond, Oath of office, and commission should the notary public

file a copy of the bond and Oath of office with the Department?

a. 15 days

b. 30 days

c. 45 days

d. 90 days

Answer D

In general, the notary public must file a copy of the bond, Oath of office, and commission with the recorder of deeds within 90 days.

16. What is the fee for administering an oath or affirmation?

a. $3

b. $4

c. $5

d. $7

Answer C

The fee for administering an Oath or affirmation (per individual taking an Oath or affirmation) is $5.

17. What is the fee for attesting or witnessing a signature?

a. $3

b. $4

c. $5

d. $7

Answer C

The fee for witnessing or attesting a signature (per signature) is $5.

18. What is the application fee when applying for an appointment as a notary public in PA?

a. $25

b. $30

c. $42

d. $48

Answer C

The application fee for a commission as a notary public is $42. It is a non-refundable fee payable to the Commonwealth of Pennsylvania.

19. After being appointed as a notary public, within how many days should the individual record the Oath of office and commission and obtain the bond with the office of the recorder of deeds?

a. Seven days

b. 15 days

c. 30 days

d. 45 days

Answer D

Prior to initiating duties as a notary public, the individual must record the Oath of office and commission with the recorder of deeds within 45 days.

20. After recording the bond, Oath of office, and commission, within how many days should a copy of the bond and Oath of office be filed with the Department?

a. 15 days

b. 30 days

c. 60 days

d. 90 days

Answer D

Within 90 days of recording the bond, Oath of office,

and commission, a copy of the bond and Oath of office must be filed with the Department.

Practice Test #5

1. What is the monetary penalty on a notary public for each act or omission that constitutes a violation of RULONA?

a. $200

b. $400

c. $750

d. $1,000

Answer D

When there is a violation of RULONA, the Department will impose a penalty of up to $1,000 on the notary public for each act or omission.

2. If a person pretends to be a notary public officer and performs notarial acts in PA, he can be accused of a?

a. Felony

b. Misdemeanor

c. Wilful neglect

d. Infraction

Answer B

Pretending to be a notary officer and conducting notarial acts is a crime. This can result in a charge of a misdemeanor. In addition, the use of a notary stamp by an authorized person is also a crime.

3. When a notary public acts fraudulently or deceitfully, he or she can be charged with what type of crime?

a. Misdemeanor

b. Felony

c. Willful neglect

d. Infraction

Answer B

Fraudulent acts or deceit on the part of the notary public can lead to a charge of a felony.

4. Prior to performing an electronic notarial act for the first time, the notary public should first?

a. Ask the Department for approval

b. Consult with the client to determine if it is okay

c. Notify the county clerk where the business is located

d. Perform a preliminary practice run on a family member

Answer A

Prior to performing any electronic notarial act, the notary first needs approval from the Department. The type of equipment used will need to be in compliance with the requirements of the State.

5. If an applicant was previously denied a notary public commission in another state, what are his chances of becoming commissioned in PA?

a. Never

b. Maybe

c. Depends on the Secretary of the Commonwealth

d. Can be commissioned if the denial was more than five years ago

Answer A

In general, if an individual has been denied a notary commission in one state, it is unlikely that he or she will be approved to work as a notary public in Pa.

6. After the appointment as a notary public, who is responsible for approving a surety bond for the individual?

a. Local county clerk

b. Office of the recorded of deeds

c. Department

d. Insurance company

Answer C

The surety bond is approved by the Department. The notary needs to obtain a bond worth $10,000- this is not an insurance policy.

7. All applicants for appointment as a notary public must submit a _____ history with the application.

a. Financial

b. Credit

c. Criminal

d. Health

Answer C

All applicants have to submit their criminal history when applying for a notary commission in Pa. Even if the individual was found not guilty of a crime, this has to be disclosed.

8. In general, once commissioned as a notary public in the Commonwealth, the individual can?

a. Not draft legal records

b. Only offer legal advice

c. Only offer legal opinion

d. Only perform legal acts if he or she works with an attorney

Answer A

In general, a notary cannot work as a lawyer or offer an opinion or even legal advice on legal matters.

9. What is the current status of notary public and

immigration?

a. The notary public should not act as an immigration consultant

b. The notary public can only give opinions on immigration matters

c. The notary public can only charge a minimum fee for his services

d. The notary public should obtain consent from the client before offering a legal consultation

Answer A

The law is simple- a notary public should not pretend to be a lawyer or offer any advice on legal matters, including immigration.

10. What is the role of the notary public when it comes to matters related to immigration in the Commonwealth?

a. Can only provide a legal opinion

b. Can only provide legal advice

c. Is not authorized to conduct any business related to immigration

d. Can only offer legal advice to friends and family

Answer C

A commission as a notary public does not authorize the notary to represent a person in a judicial or administrative proceeding relating to immigration to the United States or United States citizenship.

11. Is a notary public permitted to advertise notarial services?

a. No

b. Yes

c. Only in print form

d. Only in English

Answer B

A notary public may advertise that he offers notarial services. In such a case, the notary must include in the advertisement a required prescribed statement regarding the limits of the services and that the notary is not an attorney.

12. When can the term 'notario publico' be used by the notary public?

a. Only in advertisements

b. Only when offering immigration advice

c. Never

d. Only if he or she does not charge any fees for legal consults

Answer C

A notary public who is not an attorney may not use the term "notario" or notario publico."

13. Acting in the Commonwealth as a notary public, the law of the land confers how much immunity to public officials?

a. Limited

b. None

c. Complete

d. Depends on the violation

Answer B

A commission to act as a notary public does not provide a notary public any immunity or benefit conferred by the law of this Commonwealth on public officials or employees.

14. In order to practice as a notary public in PA, the official signature of the individual has to be registered with the?

a. Secretary of state

b. Prothonotary's office in the same county

c. Controller of deeds

d. State Department

Answer B

The official signature of each notary public shall be registered, for a fee of $0.50, in the "Notary Register" provided for that purpose in the prothonotary's office of the county where the notary public maintains an office.

15. After being appointed as a NEW notary public, within what time should the individual register his signature?

a. Seven days

b. Fourteen days

c. 30 days

d. 45 days

Answer D

After a new appointment as a notary public, the individual should register the signature within 45 days.

16. When did Rulona become effective in PA?

a. 2011

b. 2012

c. 2013

d. 2014

Answer C

RULONA became effective in 2013

17. Each notarial act should be recorded in what order?

a. By date

b. By time

c. By the day of the week

d. By the type of notarial act

Answer A

The entry in the journal has to be in a chronological fashion- starting with the date of the notarial act. In addition, all pages have to be numbered consecutively.

18. Regarding the notary journal, a notary officer in the Commonwealth can

a. Only have a tangible record

b. Only have an electronic record

c. Can have both tangible and electronic records

d. Can not have a notary journal

Answer C

In the Commonwealth of Pennsylvania, the notary public is permitted to have both electronic and a tangible or paper-based journal.

19. If the notary public violates rules and regulations set by the commission, who is liable for the damages to the client?

a. Secretary of State

b. County where the notary public practices

c. The bond issuing entity

d. The employer of the notary public

Answer C

When a notary violates the law, the damages are usually paid out by the bond-issuing entity. The money has to be repaid by the notary.

20. When a notary maintains a notary journal, he or she can?

a. Share it with others

b. Share it with the employer

c. Do not share it with anyone

d. Only share it with the office workers

Answer C

The notary journal is the exclusive property of the notary officer. It cannot be given to anyone or shared with anyone.

Practice Test #6

1. If an individual has been convicted of a misdemeanor, he or she can:

a. Only be a notary public if the misdemeanor was minor

b. Write to the Secretary of State to review his/her case

c. Become a notary public if the misdemeanor was more than five years ago

d. Become a notary public if he only has one misdemeanor

Answer B

While one cannot become a notary public if convicted of a felony. One may be able to with a misdemeanor. It all depends on the seriousness of the crime. Only the Secretary of State can make that determination.

2. A notary public works for an insurance company. On

the days he/she is off work, who can he delegate to continue with the notarizations?

a. Only his supervisor

b. Only his secretary

c. Anyone who works under him/her

d. No one

Answer D

The rule is that the notary public cannot delegate his responsibilities to any other person. It is illegal and can result in a loss of commission.

3. What is the term called for a contract between a landlord and tenant that gives the latter the right to reside in the property for a fixed period of time?

a. Lease

b. Booking

c. Tenure

d. Residency

Answer A

A lease is a formal legal contract between a landlord and tenant; it gives the tenant permission to reside in the property for a specified period of time.

4. What is the name of the instrument that ensures that one's assets will be distributed as stated after death?

a. Deed

b. Will

c. Pledge

d. Promise

Answer B

When a will is written, it ensures that the estate will be distributed according to the wishes of the decedent- the

Will overrides many legal provisions on how the estate should be distributed.

5. When a notary public has a pecuniary interest in a transaction, he or she:

a. Can continue to function as a notary public

b. Is not allowed to perform notarial acts

c. Should have a witness present during the sign-in process

d. Should consult with a lawyer

Answer B

In general, if a notary public has a pecuniary interest in a transaction, he or she should not perform any notarial act.

6. A new notary has been charged with making a forged seal. What punishment can he face?

a. Can have the commission revoked

b. Be charged in criminal court

c. Can be sued for damages in a civil court

d. All of the above

Answer D

Forgery is a serious crime and is associated with a range of penalties. In most cases, the notary public commission will be revoked, and the individual will be charged in criminal court. Any individual harmed as a result of this action can also sue the notary public in civil court.

7. A notary public shares office space with a college friend of his, who is a lawyer. How should the notary public function?

a. Offer legal advice only on matters that he knows well

b. Split the fees with his colleague

c. Can state that he has good knowledge of the law to his clients

d. Avoid the practice of law

Answer D

The best advice is for a notary public not to practice law or give out any legal advice. It is taboo to practice law without qualifications in NYS.

8. When a disbarred notary public continues to provide notarial services, he can be guilty of a:

a. Felony

b. Willful neglect

c. Infraction

d. Misdemeanor

Answer D

After being disbarred, a notary public should cease

working as a notary public. Doing so can lead to a misdemeanor.

9. Which of the following is a function of a notary public in PA?

a. Prepare a mortgage document

b. Edit a will and attach a codicil

c. Officiate a funeral

d. None of the above

Answer D

A notary public is not allowed to do any of the above. In addition, the notary public should not pretend to practice law or even give out legal advice.

10. Which of the following is NOT true about an application for a notary public?

a. The applicant can be an illegal immigrant

b. The applicant must be a resident of the commonwealth

c. The applicant can be a permanent resident

d. The applicant should have a place of business in PA

Answer A

To apply for a notary public, one can be a US citizen or permanent resident. At the time of appointment, however, the notary public has to be a US citizen. Illegal immigrants cannot apply to become a notary public in PA.

11. A notary public who moves out of State is deemed to be a resident of a PA County provided he:

a. Visits PA every month

b. Has family who lives in PA

c. Has a driver's license from PA

d. Has a business office in PA

Answer D

Even if a notary public moves out of State, as long as he or she maintains an office in PA, he can practice as a notary public. Once the office is closed, then the notary term becomes invalid.

12. Once an individual is removed as a notary public by the Secretary of State, is he or she eligible for reappointment in the future?

a. No

b. Yes

c. Only after review by the county clerk

d. Only after a review by the Secretary of State

Answer A

In general, once a notary public has been removed from office, he/she is not eligible for reappointment.

13. When a notary public commits fraud with intent to harm others, he or she is:

a. Not liable for damages to others

b. Is liable for damages to others as a result of his actions

c. Is immune from litigation

d. Is protected by the Secretary of State

Answer B

A notary public is liable to all parties that may be injured or suffer damages as a result of his or her actions.

14. When an ordinary individual pretends to act as a notary public, he or she can be guilty of a:

a. Felony

b. Misdemeanor

c. Infraction

d. Wilful neglect

Answer B

An individual not commissioned as a notary public but acts as one can be guilty of a misdemeanor.

15. A written law passed by a legislative body is known as a?

a. Statute

b. Attestation

c. Affirmation

d. Jurat

Answer A

When a legislative body passes a written law, this is known as a statute.

16. A 69-year-old dies in a motor vehicle accident but has no will. His estate goes to the probate court, where a person is appointed to manage the estate. This individual is known as the:

a. Beneficiary

b. Trustee

c. Trustor

d. Executor

Answer D

In the absence of a will, the probate court will usually appoint a person to manage the assets. This individual is known as an executor or a personal representative.

17. What is the name of the individual who signs the affidavit and swears to the accuracy of the statements made in the document?

a. Executor

b. Lessee

c. Affiant

d. Notary public

Answer C

An affiant is an individual who is the author of an affidavit. This individual first swears to the accuracy and truth of the statements made in the affidavit.

18. A document that can change or alter the provisions in a Will and be attached to the Will is known as a:

a. Affirmation

b. Codicil

c. Contract

d. Title

Answer B

In general, one is not permitted to make major changes to a will if errors are spotted or the Will needs an upgrade. In such scenarios, one can add a codicil. A codicil allows for any change, alteration, or deletion to the provisions listed in the Will. The codicil is then attached to the Will- it has to be signed and dated.

19. What is the meaning of the word 'attests?'

a. Confirm

b. Witness

c. Promise

d. Certify

Answer B

The term attests means to witness. One can witness the execution of a written document at the request of the individual who authored the document.

20. What is the name of the term when the document legally transfers property ownership from the seller to the buyer?

a. Deed

b. Bill of Sale

c. Invoice

d. Title

Answer B

The Bill of Sale is a document that transfers ownership of property or any item from the seller to the buyer. It acts as a sales receipt.

Practice Test #7

1. What is it called when an individual provides testimony out of court under oath before an officer; this testimony may be used at a trial.

a. Deposition

b. Disposition

c. Sublimation

d. Evidence

Answer A

The act of deposition usually involves providing testimony out of court in front of a notary public, lawyer, or public officer. The individual has to first take an oath, and the proceedings are recorded and can be used later in court or at a hearing.

2. The individual who establishes a trust fund is known as a:

a. Grantee

b. Grantor

c. Beneficiary

d. Recipient

Answer B

The creator of the trust fund is known as the grantor. The trust allows for the legal transfer of assets to the trustee, who will distribute the assets according to the wishes of the grantor.

3. What type of crime is punishable by a prison sentence that is usually more than a year?

a. Misdemeanor

b. Wilful neglect

c. Felony

d. Infraction

Answer C

In most felony cases, the prison sentence is over a year. With a misdemeanor, the sentence is usually less than a year.

4. What is the term called when a bank or lender has placed a legal claim against a property for an unpaid mortgage?

a. Lien

b. Outstanding Bill

c. Security

d. Encumbrance

Answer A

A lien is a legal claim against a property; it is usually placed by a creditor for unpaid bills. Liens are commonly placed against homes and cars until the owner pays up. If the debt is unpaid, the property can be auctioned, or the home can be foreclosed.

5. What is it called when an individual provides a written statement that he is giving another person the power to act on his behalf?

a. Will

b. Trust

c. Power of attorney

d. Guardianship

Answer C

A power of attorney is a legal document that gives an individual permission to act on behalf of the author.

6. What is the term called when a notary public makes a formal statement that a certain bill of exchange for payment on a certain date was refused?

a. Rejection

b. Outstanding

c. Overdue

d. Protest

Answer D

A protest is a formal statement in writing by the notary public. It is usually written when a certain bill or promissory note on a specified date is presented and is either accepted or refused.

7. Recently, a notary public was removed from office because of perjury. When can he reapply for the same position?

a. Only after seven years

b. After retaking the exam in 2 years

c. Never

d. After submitting letters of support to the Secretary of State

Answer C

Once a notary public has been removed from office, it is impossible to get reinstated. The removal is permanent.

8. What is the term called when the Minister of Foreign Affairs confirms that the documents have been obtained legally and issues a Specialized certificate?

a. Affidavit

b. Apostille

c. Chapeau

d. Amendment

Answer B

An apostille refers to a specialized certificate that is usually issued by the foreign ministry or consular service. The apostille confirms that the documents have been obtained in a legal manner- allowing them to be recognized in other nations.

9. What is the term called when someone is allowed to make a solemn declaration because he or she conscientiously objects to taking an oath?

a. Addendum

b. Affirmation

c. Refutation

d. Denial

Answer B

In law, some people may not want to take the oath for a variety of reasons. These individuals can then make a solemn declaration when they conscientiously object to taking the oath.

10. The supplementary document that allows you to

make edits to the Will and attach it to the Will is known as the:

a. Papier

b. Deed

c. Last testament

d. Codicil

Answer D

The codicil is a legal document that acts as a supplement to the Will. Since one is not allowed to make major changes to the written Will, one can make a supplementary copy with the edits and attach it to the Will.

11. What is it called when an individual makes a formal statement outside the court but in the presence of a lawyer and promises to tell the truth?

a. Disposition

b. Deposition

c. Description

d. Distribution

Answer B

A deposition is a formal statement that an individual makes out of the courtroom to a notary or a public officer. First, he or she has to take an oath, and the statements are recorded to be used later in court or at a hearing.

12. Which of the following errors can lead to the invalidity of a notarized instrument?

a. If the notary public is working outside his jurisdiction

b. Misspelling the name of the notary public

c. Working with an expired term of commission

d. All of the above

Answer D

Some unintentional errors that can lead to the invalidity of a notarized document include jurisdiction issues, misspellings, expired term, having no business address, and ineligibility.

13. In general, a notary public should not:

a. Give advice on legal matters

b. Not ask for legal referrals

c. Not advertise that he or she is a legal professional

d. All of the above

Answer D

When it comes to legal matters, the best advice for a notary public is to avoid the subject. Advice or opinion on legal matters is also not permitted. The State takes it very seriously when notary publics pretend to act like lawyers.

14. In general, a notary public should never acknowledge which document?

a. Passport application

b. Loan document

c. Rental application

d. Will

Answer D

The general rule is that a notary public should never acknowledge a will. This is best left to the lawyers.

15. What is the name of the certificate that is usually issued by the State Department that permits international usage of the documents?

a. Visa

b. Apostille

c. Passport

d. Permit

Answer B

An apostille is a certificate that is usually issued by the State Department. This certificate proves the authenticity of official documents/papers that can be used abroad.

16. What does it mean when an individual has an apostille?

a. He can use it instead of a passport to travel

b. He or she has a prior criminal conviction

c. He has access to the safe deposit box in the bank

d. He has certified documents for international use

Answer D

An apostille refers to a specialized certificate that is usually issued by the foreign ministry or consular service. The apostille confirms that the documents have been obtained in a legal manner- allowing them to be recognized in other nations.

17. Which word is often used interchangeably with deponent?

a. Defendant

b. Plaintiff

c. Affiant

d. Executor

Answer C

Deponent is often used interchangeably with affiant.

18. What are the minimum age requirements to become a notary public in PA?

a. 16

b. 18

c. 20

d. Can be of any age

Answer B

The minimum age for an application for a Notary public in PA is 18

19. The notary public's stamp will usually not contain the following information?

a. The notary public ID number

b. The expiration of the commission

c. The words 'Notary Public'

d. The notary public's business address

Answer D

The physical address of the notary public is never found on the stamp.

20. When a notary public is suspended, what should happen to the stamping device?

a. The notary public should destroy it

b. The notary public should store it in a safe place

c. The notary public should surrender the device to the State

d. The notary public should give it back to the employer

Answer C

When the notary public is suspended, or the commission is revoked, the stamping device should be surrendered to the State.

Practice Test #8

1. Following termination of employment, what should the notary public do with the notary journal?

a. Surrender it to the employer

b. Keep it safe

c. Send it back to the county clerk

d. Destroy it

Answer B

If the notary public resigns or the employment is terminated, he or she should ensure that the notary journal is safe and secure. It should not be handed over to the employer or anyone else.

2. Once the candidate has passed the exam, before he or she can practice as a notary public, under RULONA, what amount of surety bond must be obtained?

a. $2,000

b. $4,000

c. $7,000

d. $10,000

Answer D

Under RULONA an applicant for a commission has to first obtain a surety bond from a licensed and approved insurer in PA in the order of the amount of $10K

3. If a notary public's commission is revoked, he or she must deliver the journal to the recorder of deeds within

a. Two days

b. Ten days

c. 15 days

d. 30 days

Answer D

Upon expiration, resignation, or revocation of commission, the notary must deliver the journal to the recorder of Deeds in the county in which they work within 30 Days

4. When the notary public's commission has expired, the seal should be?

a. Returned to the Department

b. Given back to the employer

c. Destroyed

d. Kept in a safe place

Answer C

Once the commission has expired, the notary seal should be destroyed so that no one else can ever use it.

5. Which of the following is usually not documented in the notary journal?

a. Type of notarial act

b. The identification of the individual

c. The notary fee

d. The city location of the client

Answer D

The city location of the notary public is usually not documented in the notary journal.

6. When can a notary public refuse to perform a notarial act?

a. When the competency of the signer is in question

b. When there appears to be a non-voluntary signature

c. When there is a mismatch between the person and the photo ID

d. All of the above

Answer D

Sometimes, a notary officer may decline to perform a notarial service; this usually occurs when the competency of the signer is in question, the signature appears to be non-voluntary, and there is a mismatch between the photo ID and the physical appearance of the person.

7. If the notary public loses the notary journal, when should he notify the Department of State?

a. Within 5 days

b. Promptly

c. Within 30 days

d. After first searching for it for a week

Answer B

In general, if the notary journal is lost or stolen, the notary officer should notify the Department immediately or as soon as possible.

8. To be an e-notary in the Commonwealth, the officer should:

a. Use tamper-proof electronic technology

b. Use at least two antivirus programs

c. Only communicate with encrypted language

d. Use a reputable internet server

Answer A

When using electronic technology for notarization, it is vital that the device and programs be tamper-proof. One has to buy the device from a reputable vendor and ensure that the system complies with the State requirements.

9. Which of the following is not a requirement for becoming a notary public in PA?

a. Be at least 18 years of age

b. Be a US citizen

c. Have at minimum a college degree

d. Read and write English

Answer C

There are no formal education requirements to become a notary public in Pa. however, the applicant must be able to read and write in English.

10. Which of the following is not exempt from working as a notary public?

a. Holder of a judicial office

b. A federal employee

c. Member of the general assembly

d. An individual authorized by the law of the tribe

Answer D

An individual authorized by the law of the tribe to perform a notarial act

11. The name change can be done for free in the Commonwealth as long as it is done within how many days of the change?

a. Seven days

b. Fourteen days

c. 21 days

d. 30 days

Answer D

If the notary public makes a name change, he or she should notify the Department within 30 days of the name change. This request should be made either in writing or electronically.

12. Following a resignation, a notary public should deliver the rubber stamp to the Dept of State Bureau of Commissions within how many days?

a. Three days

b. Five days

c. Ten days

d. 30 days

Answer C

Following the resignation, the notary public should deliver the stamp to the State within ten days.

13. Which of the following is not usually found on the official notary stamp?

a. The words 'Commonwealth of Pennsylvania'

b. The name, 'Notario Publico'

c. The expiration date of the commission

d. The commission ID number

Answer B

The official notary stamp does contain the words Notary Public in English only.

14. The security of the stamping device rests solely with the?

a. Employer

b. Notary public

c. Department

d. Insurer

Answer B

The onus of looking after the stamping device rests with the notary officer. The seal has to be stored in a secure and locked place so no one can have access to it.

15. Following the death of the notary officer, the notary seal should not be?

a. Destroyed

b. Defaced

c. Rendered unusable

d. Surrendered to the Department

Answer D

Following the death of the notary public, the seal should be rendered unusable by destroying, defacing, or damaging it. It is only surrendered when the notary officer has been suspended or the commission has been revoked.

16. How much is the administrative penalty when a notary officer intentionally misleads a client?

a. $200

b. $500

c. $750

d. $1,000

Answer D

The administrative penalty for intentional errors can be up to $1,000.

17. Which of the following is not a prohibitive act on the part of the notary public?

a. Placing an advertisement

b. Giving out legal advice

c. Using the terms 'notario publico'

d. Giving an opinion on immigration matters to a client

Answer A

A notary public can advertise as long as he also has a disclaimer that states that he or she is not a lawyer and cannot give legal advice.

18. When a notary officer suddenly dies, within what time should the personal representative return the notary journal to the Recorder of Deeds?

a. Seven days

b. Fourteen days

c. 21 days

d. 30 days

Answer D

In general, the personal representative has 30 days within which to return the notary journal following the death of the notary officer.

19. When a notary marries and changes her name, within what time frame should the change be reported to the Department?

a. Seven days

b. Fifteen days

c. 21 days

d. 30 days

Answer D

All name changes have to be reported to the State within 30 days. The same applies to an address change.

20. When a notary officer in PA resigns, where should the letter of resignation be sent?

a. Mayor's office

b. Recorder of Deeds

c. Dept of State Bureau of Commissions

d. The employer

Answer C

The letter of resignation should be submitted to the

Dept of State Bureau of Commissions, Elections, and Legislation. The letter should be sent within 30 days from the date of resignation.

Practice Test #9

1. When a notary officer resigns, the stamp would be delivered to the Dept of State Bureau of Commissions within how many days?

a. Seven days

b. Ten days

c. 21 days

d. 30 days

Answer B

Following a resignation, the notary officer should deliver the letter to the Dept of State Bureau of Commissions within ten days.

2. What an individual pleads no contest but yet accepts the court's punishment, this is known as

a. Guilt without association

b. Not guilty

c. Nolo contendere

d. Nolle prosequi

Answer C

There are instances when an individual will plead no contest or nolo contendere- meaning the person does not admit to guilt but yet accepts the punishments given out by the court.

3. Following reappointment, the notary officer has to register his signature with the prothonotary's office of the county where the business is located within how many days?

a. Ten days

b. Fifteen days

c. 30 days

d. 45 days

Answer D

Following reappointment, the notary has to register his or her signature with the prothonotary's office in the county where the business is located within 45 days.

4. As per the Commonwealth of PA, when it comes to notary publics, the term conviction means:

a. A guilty verdict in court

b. A not guilty verdict as a result of a mental illness

c. A plea of no contest

d. All of the above

Answer D

In the Commonwealth, a conviction does not necessarily mean a sentence imposed by the court. Even a not guilty verdict as a result of a mental illness is deemed to be a conviction.

5. An electronic signature may include which of the following:

a. Electronic sound

b. Electronic symbol

c. Electronic process

d. All of the above

Answer D

An electronic signature can take many forms and can include a sound, symbol, or some type of process.

6. The notary journal is the exclusive property of the?

a. Department of State

b. Recorder of Deeds

c. Secretary of the Commonwealth

d. Notary officer

Answer D

The notary journal belongs solely to the notary officer. It cannot be given to anyone. Even if the employer has paid for the journal, he or she cannot ask for the journal.

7. A new notary public in PA has been asked to act as an immigration expert for his community. What should he do?

a. Only offer advice

b. Offer to answer question

c. Deny the request

d. Only charge a small fee

Answer C

The law is clear; a notary public is not a lawyer and should refrain from offering advice or opinions on legal matters.

8. What is the meaning of the word 'promulgate?'

a. Promise

b. Promote

c. Persevere

d. Pretend

Answer B

Promulgate means to advance or promote an idea or make something known.

9. Which of the following is not listed as a notarial act in

a. Noting a protest of negotiable instrument

b. Taking a verification on oath

c. Witnessing or attesting a signature

d. Certifying immigration papers

Answer D

A notary is not permitted to undertake any legal duties that also include immigration matters.

10. In which of the following scenarios is a notary officer prohibited from performing a notarial act?

a. The notary officer's wife has a pecuniary interest

b. Where the notary officer is a stakeholder of a publicly traded company that is a party to transaction

c. The notary officer is an employee of a corporate party

d. The notary officer's fees are not contingent on the transaction

Answer A

A notarial officer is not permitted to perform any type of notarial act when he or the spouse has any direct pecuniary interest.

11. For a government ID to be valid, it must:

a. Contain the signature of the client

b. Have a photograph

c. Is current

d. All of the above

Answer D

All government IDs used for identification purposes must be current, have a photograph, and/or have a signature. The photo ID must be satisfactory in order to be accepted as sufficient proof.

12. To be a notary officer in the Commonwealth of PA, the individual:

a. Can reside out of State as long as he regularly visits PA

b. Must be a resident of the state

c. Can reside out of State but must be married to a resident of PA

d. Can marry in PA but can then reside out of State

Answer B

To be a notary public, the individual must be a resident of the Commonwealth.

13. All notary publics renewing their commission need to?

a. Retake the exam

b. Complete the 3-hour basic public education course

c. Pass an English reading and writing course

d. Re-apply a year in advance

Answer B

All notary officers seeking a reappointment need to take the 3-hour basic public education course- there are no exceptions.

14. What is the duration of the notary public exam?

a. 15 mins

b. 30 mins

c. 60 mins

d. 120 mins

Answer C

The notary exam is 60 mins in duration; one needs a score of at least 75 to pass.

15. What is the term for a certification by a notary public that a negotiable instrument formally presented for payment has been dishonored?

a. Rollback

b. Protest

c. Codicil

d. YOU

Answer B

A protest is a certification by a notary that an instrument formally presented for payment was dishonored.

16. In general, who usually will request for the notary public to protest?

a. Lawyers

b. Financial institutions

c. Healthcare providers

d. Tenants

Answer B

Financial institutions- i.e., banks and lenders often request notary public officers to protest on their behalf.

17. In Pennsylvania, how many notarial acts is a notary public authorized to perform?

a. 3

b. 4

c. 5

d. 6

Answer D

The notary public is allowed to perform six notarial acts. 1) take an acknowledgment 2) administer an oath and affirmation 3) take a verification on oath or affirmation (includes an affidavit) 4) witness or attest a signature 5) certify or attest a copy or deposition and 6) note a protest of a negotiable instrument.

18. To become an e-notary, the applicant should:

a. Need to retake the notary exam

b. Already be a commissioned officer

c. Take the 3-hour basic public education course

d. Pass a basic computer test

Answer B

To be an e-notary, the only requirement is that the individual already be a notary public. There are no additional requirements.

19. Are notary public officers allowed to certify a transcript of a deposition?

a. Yes

b. No

c. Depends on whether it is a civil or criminal matter

Answer A

Yes, a notary public can certify a transcript of a deposition.

Made in the USA
Middletown, DE
12 November 2023

42489861R00146